A WAY OUT

A WAY OUT

Nancy Hannan

Editorial development and creative design support by Ascent:
www.itsyourlifebethere.com

This book is dedicated to
my children,
who have given my life
purpose, meaning and joy

God, whose law it is, that he who learns must suffer.
And even in our sleep, pain that cannot forget,
falls drop by drop upon the heart,
and in our own despite, and against our will,
comes wisdom to us, by the awful grace of God...

— A E S C H Y L U S

INTRODUCTION

THIS IS NOT THE BOOK I intended to write, but when my coach/editor, David Hazard, read a portion of the book I *was* writing, he greatly encouraged me to write *this* one, instead.

"This book has the power to help others," he said. "So many people are trapped and do not know how to get out. You found the way, and can show them the way out. "I had no idea what he was talking about, but he came up with an outline and I just began to write.

That meant I would have to revisit the past...go back into my childhood, and the years leading up to, and including, my thirty year marriage.

What I found my "way out of," was years of abuse. A few years before my marriage, a life altering experience totally changed me, left me hurting. But I finally managed to rise above it to find peace, wholeness, and a spirituality that went beyond my Catholic upbringing.

Before the experience, I was a happy, open, cheerful person. I laughed a lot, was a good nurse, and loved my work. Though mostly reserved, I could be outgoing. I made friends easily and loved a party. I would take a risk if challenged and was willing to accept the consequences. I was self-confident and as the oldest of eight children was comfortable being in charge. I also considered myself a good and practicing Catholic.

For three years after the experience, I appeared to be my old self to the world, but inside, I knew better. I was no longer the person I used to be. I was different. When my health returned, I went back to work and began to date the man I would eventually marry.

It was only after the marriage, that the transformation became apparent.

At first, I was happy in the marriage, but soon discovered that I could not stand up for myself when I needed to. I was incapable of being who I once was. That person was trapped inside me, and the toxic view I had of myself trapped me in this marriage.

The book is about me, not the people in it. I will show the reader how that view of myself changed and how it set me free.

I found in writing the book that I needed to look at those who have contributed to the pain in my life with compassion and forgiveness. Only by doing this, could I elevate the pain of the past to something of meaning.

My parents were a product of their own upbringing. They raised a large family using discipline and order that one might find, in todays world, bordering on abusive. I am sure their intention was not to harm us but to make sure we were as God-fearing as they were. However, that intense indoctrination had negative effects on some of us.

I grew up in the shadow of the Great Depression, still, we always had food on the table, heat in the house, clothes on our backs and we went to Catholic grade school and High School.

We were taught manners and saw our parents interact in a positive way within the community and the Church. They were compassionate to a fault, with outsiders.

We did not realize we were poor, but understood that we could not afford what some of our friends with fewer siblings had.

My husband was a good man and came from a good family or I would not have married him. He had an excellent reputation as a surgeon and many of his patients were physicians. Not only was he charming, he had a delightful personality. He never seemed concerned about money and was always generous. I was very proud of him those early years.

But shortly after our marriage, I began to see a distinctly different personality emerge in my husband. I got a brief glimpse of it only once in the three and one half years before we married.

Because of the underlying vision I had of myself, I was unable to confront his behavior effectively. I settled into a life of control and subservience. Always looking for answers and a way to change my life, I continued to pray to God who I thought had abandoned me. I always believed that things would get better, if only I could find the answers.

I hope, as you travel these pages with me, you will find ways to avert any future unhappiness in your own lives by seeing where I went wrong, and what I could have done differently. And if you already are where you do not want to be, you will find that there is a way out...if you believe in yourself and have faith in your own capacity and ability to honor the person you really are.

Guilt and fear are known motivators, but we should be motivated by something more honorable. When we are driven by the desires and demands of another, whether it be a person or a business, we devalue ourselves.

As an individual, we have a right to our own opinions and our own belief system as long as they do not interfere with the rights of another. We have a right to demand the respect we have earned. And we have a right to be free to function as we see fit, again, as long as it dos not interfere with the rights and welfare of another.

There were many positive aspects in both my childhood and my marriage, and I am grateful for those good things and the good times. I am equally grateful for the opportunity that life has given me for the lessons I needed to learn.

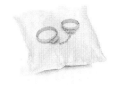

CHAPTER 1

AS WE FINISHED the sumptuous breakfast my friend, Claire, had fixed for the four of us, I was completely unsuspecting. My husband, Charles, was his usual charming self. Claire and her husband, Dan, laughed at his good humor. I smiled at the way my friends and my husband had connected so well. I'd finished my plate quickly, because there were things I had to do before we left Philadelphia for our home outside Washington, DC that morning.

Leaving the table, I fed our three-month-old baby, then gathered our things together. Claire had watched Cara, so Charles and I could attend my sister's wedding the day before in nearby Philadelphia. It had been a great weekend and the first time we had traveled with the baby.

Claire, Dan and I had been good friends when I'd lived in Philadelphia the two years before I started to date Charles, and I loved visiting them now in their gorgeous home. They stood for us when we got married at City Hall just eighteen months before. Dan had a lucrative legal practice in the city and Claire was a fun, free spirit and one of my best friends. It had been good to see them both again, I thought, as we loaded our things and baby Cara into the car, then kissed them goodbye.

Anyone looking at us would have thought we were two ideal couples with bright futures ahead. From surface appearance, you would never have known the unpleasant truth about my marriage.

Driving home a little later that Sunday morning in December, Charles and I talked about the wedding and family and other things—events coming up at the country club Charles had joined the year before we got married.

Once, when a comical situation came up, he laughed that infectious laugh of his which always made me laugh along with him. I looked over at him, and saw, for a moment, the old Charles, the man I'd married a year and one half ago. He was just at six feet tall, trim, muscular, an athlete and in good shape physically. He was handsome and with his short-cropped grey hair, looked the part of a distinguished physician. He had many friends and was well liked by them. This morning he was in his old, cheerful mood.

On the other hand, I found myself a little nervous. First, I'd begun to feel a bit queasy—carsick perhaps—or maybe I had eaten breakfast too quickly. But it was more than physical unease.

Charles' good moods had become rare since the baby was born. She was colicky and her fitfulness made him anxious. The miles passed, and my unsettledness continued and, from time to time I glanced over my shoulder at Cara, asleep in the backseat. Her eyes remained closed, her perfect little face calm. Would she stay asleep...or wake and cry...unsettling the peaceful atmosphere?

Charles remarked, "You're awfully quiet." I looked over at him. "What are you thinking about?" he said.

I was not ready to tell him what was weighing on me. "I was just thinking about our trip to Charleston next spring with Cara and hoping she will be this good then, it's going to be a long drive and she'll be teething by then, you know."

"Oh, I thought you were thinking about your old boyfriend back here in Philadelphia."

The transformation was beginning. I looked at him out of the corner of my eye and saw the smirk on his face. He had just opened a painful wound that was taking a long time to heal and this was cruel, almost sadistic...my answer seemed to still his jealousy, at least for the moment.

Left with an uneasy silence in the air, I thought about the awful gap that opened up between us. It was troubling and mystifying. Whether I had gone to Philadelphia by myself to visit Claire or if he and I had gone together, Charles would always make reference to my 'old boyfriend'. I thought that after Cara was born, it would stop, but it did not. All I knew was that every time it happened, I felt pain, and then the pain would turn to anger. I was tired of having my past thrown in my face. There was a reason I felt it necessary to share this one incident with him before we married, and at that time he told me it did not matter, we would forget it and never bring it up again. But he continued to do so.

Once, I asked him if we could talk about why he kept bringing up a subject, long over, that he knew bothered me. "It bothers you? Well it bothers me that you were with another man before me."

Charles had found my Achilles heel. He seemed to delight in bringing up a subject that he knew was hurtful to me.

In the beginning I thought that he would get over his jealousy, and, with time, would stop referring to my past. It did not take long to realize that the more I made him aware of my displeasure with his words or actions, the more he used them. I soon learned how futile it was to tell him that certain behavior bothered me, for instead of appealing to his sense of caring, I was giving him ammunition.

While he appeared the same, something about Charles had begun to change and I could not put my finger on it. Before we'd married, and before Cara was born, I'd never found him to be an anxious person. As a physician he had to be strong and steady; in the operating room he was a picture of calm. A little caustic at times—a little more so recently than when we met—but never hassled. His kindness and level-headed demeanor were characteristics I'd always liked about him. But now shades of something else had begun to show through his personality.

Pennsylvania continued to recede far behind us, as we approached suburban Washington, DC—getting nearer to home. There was another reason I wanted Cara to sleep. Something dawned on me, and I needed time for it to settle in my head. Despite my deepening unease, I kept the banter light.

I had no way of knowing that this would be the last pleasant, loving, cheerful conversation my husband and I would ever have.

Later that day, I tucked Cara into her crib in our lovely home in McLean, Virginia. We had looked forward to our first child. Charles and I were both so delighted with her. I closed Cara's door, and returned downstairs where Charles had already settled into his favorite chair to read the Sunday Washington Post. Life seemed so perfect at this moment. His medical practice was doing quite well, and we both enjoyed the country club. Golf was his thing and he especially enjoyed the socializing that was important to a developing practice. On top of that, we now had a beautiful baby daughter. We enjoyed a good social life and since many of our physician friends were from my Alma Mater, Georgetown, I knew many of them from my student days. Yes, life was good.

But not for long.

On the trip home, I recognized that my car-sickness was really the nausea of pregnancy...and our baby was only three months old. Some part of me knew my husband would not be overjoyed with the news, so I decided not to tell him...just yet.

I waited a couple more weeks to see if I got my period, but it never came. It was now four months and I knew I was pregnant, but wanted confirmation before I told my husband. I needed a doctors 'order to have the blood test done and since my husband and I had already decided I was not going back to the Dr. who delivered Cara, I would just ask him. Why did I dread asking my husband to write the order? What was I afraid of? We had talked about children, and I agreed that we would "not have a house-full like my mother and my sister," as he so nicely put it. So we will have the two close together.

It was a Saturday night and the baby was asleep as we went into the small den to watch Perry Mason, our favorite Saturday night show. Charles moved the port-a-crib that we used as a playpen over to the side of the room, and I picked up the stack of diapers I'd fold while we watched TV. "Remember when we would sit here with a glass of wine and watch TV without all this stuff in the room?" he said. "Yes, but think of what we have in place of the space now," I said, happy with my new life. He made no reply.

I waited until the show was over and he was relaxed.

When he got up to leave I stopped him..."Charles, I have not had a period since the baby was born and would like to have a pregnancy test done to make sure I am not pregnant. Since I still don't have a doctor, would you write the order?"

I spoke the words calmly, but holding my breath. His face changed and I detected a mask of rage. "You better not be pregnant! Where do you think the money will come from to educate more children?" He was earning close to $35,000/yr. and that was good money back in the early sixties. I was putting one-third of that into savings and there seemed to be sufficient left for expenses. Money should not have been the problem.

Charles stormed out of the room. I followed him upstairs, checked on the baby who was sleeping soundly, and went into our bedroom. He was pacing the floor, half yelling at me with a few expletives thrown in, then went into the bathroom, slamming the bathroom door behind him so loudly it woke Cara.

After I got her back to sleep I cautiously went into our bedroom and climbed into bed. He had his back to me and did not even say good night. I felt like I had committed a crime and was already being punished before being found guilty.

Monday morning I went to the lab, which was in his building. The day after they drew my blood, the test came back. Charles came home from the office waving the damning results at me. "Well, I hope you're happy! Is that all you know how to do, get yourself pregnant! What kind of dumb nurse would get herself pregnant right after having a baby! It's a disgrace. It's embarrassing! How can I tell my family that you are pregnant again?"

I felt that his behavior was irrational but thought if I left him alone he could let out the steam and would calm down. I was the one who would be carrying the baby and if I did not mind, why should he. Back then, I totally misread him. The problem went much deeper and it would take years for me to see it. Still, I was not able to assimilate his vindictive words and behavior into a meaningful response. Instead, I sunk deeper into a feeling of worthlessness, because in his eyes, I had done something stupid. The feeling of worthlessness was re-enforced each time he made a negative comment, which he did frequently. Sometimes his anger would be so intense that he would follow me around the house until he finished his tirade.

I had never seen this behavior in him before and could not imagine what I had done or said. I would try to get away from him but he continued to follow me and I would freeze, not knowing what to say back to him. I may have been afraid of him but had no reason to be back then.

Once, when I asked him to please," Tell me what's the matter so we can we talk about it," he simply walked away. That was his way of avoiding a discussion, and I was left to wonder. After a while I just learned to accept this behavior because I was unable to alter it, but when he raised his voice, as he did in the beginning, I was immobilized. I was once again the ten or twelve year old girl back in the living room of my childhood home, standing at attention, listening to my father, not being allowed to answer the accusations, but wanting to scream back at them both and praying they would both shut up. That feeling of helplessness had re-surfaced years later in the marriage and I was once again facing an authority figure with whom I could not argue, or so I believed.

Words and feelings from my childhood surfaced. "You should be ashamed of yourself," "Who do you think you are?" "You are just selfish." Words that I believed, because someone of authority had spoken them. This toxic belief of who I was, planted in my childhood, would undermine me and hold me prisoner for decades.

I accepted the fact there was nothing I could do to stop his harassing and demoralizing words. I did not see my own authority, I did not realize I was entitled to my opinion or that it mattered. I did not walk away from him at first, fearful of being rude and further agitating him, so I stayed and tolerated what amounted to verbal abuse. Inside, I was angry and wanted to hit him, tell him I would not be spoken to like that but I did nothing. I simply could not think of anything to do. I believed that by being passive and non-confrontational, I could defuse this aberrant behavior.

The pattern I was setting was counter-productive because he could now become belligerent at will and nothing would happen, but it only seemed like nothing happened, a lot was happening. I was processing these events inwardly. My feelings of worth were being eroded, and I believed my unhappiness and disappointment in the relationship was punishment for not only marrying out of the Church, but for another "grave sin" I had committed.

I not only felt incapable of defending myself, but believed I deserved it. Shame had been rooted in me from childhood.

CHAPTER 2

MY MOTHER'S BROTHER, Belding, was an outcast of the family. He had usurped their mother's money and then lost it during the great Depression. My mother called him *selfish*.

We all knew the story of Belding, and the terrible thing he had done. We knew he was the outcast, the evil one in the family even though none of us had ever met or seen him.

He had been branded "selfish," and it was the worst brand you could carry.

When my mother would get annoyed with me, she would use that word and some times I would not have the foggiest notion of why she would say this to me. "You are selfish! You are just like Belding." There was contempt in her voice, and my soul would shrink.

All I had done was ask if I could go somewhere with a friend or go out to play, or could I have something....I don't

recall the issues, only the word, SELFISH. I was only thinking of myself and not her need for help in the house.

I did not think I was selfish, and yet, if someone used that
word to brand me, or even hint that I had only thought of
myself, or even just acted in my own best interest, I would
feel that same shrinking feeling inside. All my strength would
collapse.

When I was five, my mother was having a difficult time
with nausea of pregnancy and often needed to stay in bed
in the mornings. My father would feed the three of us little
girls breakfast before going to work, and then leave our lunch
on the lower shelf of the fridge where I could reach it. He
would also leave something for our mother if she wanted it.
He would tell me to watch my two-year old sister, Joan and
make sure she did not run away. Joan was very strong and
would pull away from me when I tried to hold her back. And
she was *fast*.

He told me—drilled into me, in fact—"You are the oldest
and it is your responsibility to take care of the younger ones."

Mary Lou was four, and she and I managed to get food up
to Mama and corral Joan until the next door neighbor would
come over to check on us and often take the three of us back
to her house so Mama could rest.

The words, "You are the oldest and it is your responsibility..." again branded me. Like a computer that records what it
has been programmed, my soul believed what it had repeatedly been fed! If anything went wrong, it was my fault—and
I would be judged.

When my next sister, Doris, was one, I was ready for first
grade and we moved from Evarts St. in DC. to Kearney St.
near Catholic University and the Franciscan Monastery. On
Sundays, our father would take Mary Lou, Joan and me for

long walks. We either went to see how the building of the Shrine was coming along or to the Franciscan Monastery where a family friend, Brother Gerard, was a monk. At the monastery, our father would take us up the double stairs to the life-sized scene of the crucifixion. Here he would tell us that Jesus died this horrible death on the cross because of our sins. I would look at the beaten, bloody body of Jesus nailed to the cross and felt such guilt that He died for my sins, and every time we did something wrong, we were reminded of this image.

I always wanted to know more about why Jesus died and found that some things we were taught did not make sense to me. Whenever I would question anyone in authority, I would be put down and made to feel that I was wrong for asking.

In third grade I asked Sr. Frances Helen where the rest of us came from since Cain killed his brother Abel and they were the only children of Adam and Eve. She told me, "Never question the word of God again," and made me stay after school.

I may have been discouraged and ridiculed for searching for answers, but later it made me more determined.

Not only was judgment harsh back then...punishment was even harsher.

I was standing at attention in the living room with my two sisters, waiting to be chastised by our father for some minor infraction of the rules or maybe for simply upsetting our mother that day. The infractions could be as simple as getting water in your boots, or leaving a book at school, or not making your bed.

He asked us, one by one, "what did you do?"

We would answer him, "I don't know," because we often had no idea why we were standing there. We just remembered our mother telling us, "Wait until your father hears about this."

By the time I was ten or so, I would stand in that unpleasant lineup, feeling like a criminal. What could we have done that was so wrong for him to make all three of us stand here for what seemed to be forever.

I was also angry. Once, when he lashed out at one of my sisters, I interrupted him to defend her.

"You wait until I am finished," he barked. But then his voice was never soft or gentle. He was loud, firm and controlling. We are being taught a lesson, but I am learning that it is futile to try to correct or explain. It is easier to go along with him than risk being made to feel even worse.

The worst part was the inevitable yanking of his belt from its loops and the swishing of it as it lashed across our legs and bottoms.

I would look toward my mother, who was nearby, hoping she would stop him. She always looked away and continued to read her book. I felt anger toward her, as well.

"*Why don't you punish us yourself,* I would think, but did not dare to say, *especially when you know how he will do it?* I felt I could not trust her because she did not defend us.

When I have children, I told myself, *I will deal with them myself and not tell their father every little thing they have done. I will protect them and never allow anyone to make them feel bad about themselves.*

Those sessions always included the same accusation: "Mama was at death's door giving birth to each one of you and this is how you treat her!" Guilt, guilt, and more guilt... along with the lash of the belt.

But once he had our full time and attention (forced as it was), our father would further indoctrinate us into the perils of sin. Where the nuns left off, he would continue until we lived in perpetual fear of the punishing God of the Old Testament. When, at the end of the world, everyone will be lined up and any sin we ever committed will be made public. God would then decide who goes to Heaven and who goes to Hell on that Final Judgment Day.

And when our father finished, we would be sent to our rooms to "think about it."

I thought about unfairness. I thought my mother was wrong. I felt confused about God, I hoped He was kind and loving, and would not send me to hell for thinking bad thoughts especially about my parents, because bad thoughts were sins.

We were taught to respect our mother, and she demanded this herself. We were not allowed to talk back or question anything. If I ever did speak out, I could expect a very stern "Who do you think you are?" They were the ultimate authority, and not to be questioned.

As a child, I was not *asked* to do something, I was *told* to do it, and in a usually commanding voice. I suppose this was their way of raising a proper, God fearing, large family, but it did not feel right to me. I was useful. But what I thought or felt or wanted was not important to them. I felt that I, Nancy, was unimportant.

One Christmas, for example, the whole family came down to the living room that morning and there, under the beautiful Christmas tree, were all the presents.

My eye immediately went to the book, "When I Grow Up, I'll Be a Nurse." I always wanted to be a nurse because I had such wonderful role models. Autumn Perkins was our Pediatrician's nurse, and I loved her. She was not only one of my earliest role models but a good family friend. When her husband was transferred to NJ, she told my parents that she wanted me to come to Trenton that summer for a visit. I was not only delighted, but surprised that they would allow me to go. I was maybe about twelve when my parents put me on the train at Union Station, but I felt like an important adult.

I knew that book under the tree was for me. I was so excited that they remembered my saying I wanted to be a nurse when I grew up. And then I saw that my name was not on it. It was a gift for one of my sister's. When she was given the book, my sister looked at it and said, "I don't want to be a nurse."

I asked her if we could trade.

My parents had not heard my heart's desire after all. I would have to continue to remind them.

By my late teen years, they realized that I had a firm desire to be a nurse, and a means was found to send me to nursing school. The Sunday I left for Georgetown was one of the most memorable days of my life.

We were only allowed to bring one trunk and everything I owned was in it. As I moved my belongings out of the house, I had this wonderful, exuberant feeling of being free, but I would miss my four sisters and three brothers. Johnny and Tommy were eight and seven, Mike, the baby was one. Mary, Joan, Doris and Eileen were seventeen, fifteen, twelve and three, respectively.

I knew that now, when I would be studying, I would not be interrupted to change the baby's diaper, or to help one of my brothers with his homework, or put Eileen to bed, or that I would not be called away from where I was, to do something else. But I still felt very sad at leaving my two youngest siblings. They were like my own children. I literally cared for them since they were born, and felt responsible for them. I was expected to watch, feed, and bathe them and I always

put them to bed. They both called me "Mama," and I was determined to get home as often as I could to see them.

I did not realize how soon, and how often, I would be going home.

While my classmates were getting to know each other, and check out the campus on the week-ends, I had orders to go home. The Nun in charge told me that my father asked that I be allowed to come home whenever possible because "the baby won't eat and keeps crying for "Mama."

After a few of those week-ends at home the little ones settled down and accepted the fact that the woman who dressed and fed them *was* their mother. As my visits home became less frequent the two little ones seemed to adjust and I felt more at ease focusing on my studies.

At school we had a very ridged schedule and few privileges back then. We were in training for thirty-six straight months with no summers off and only two weeks vacation, which was spread over the year. While some of my classmates complained about the rigid restrictions, I did not seem to mind. I was happier than I had ever been in my life. I could be myself and made friends easily. I could act goofy without fear of criticism and we were treated with respect and as adults. No first names, I was Miss Moore.

All the while, I kept alive the image of my true role model, Mrs. Whiting. The tall, elegant nurse who replaced Autumn Perkins in the pediatrician's office had taken me under her wing the four years I worked beside her on Saturdays. I wanted to be just like her.

Life was good those three years at Georgetown and I even enjoyed the difficult affiliations. We spent three months at the old Gallinger Hospital for our communicable disease training with TB patients, three months at Seton Psychiatric Institute in Baltimore and three months at the old Children's Hospital at 14th and U St. NW.

Mainly, this was a time of regeneration for me. I had the psychic space to be myself without parental interference. Life was not easy, in fact, it was rather difficult, but it was rewarding. Student nurses were treated as persons of knowledge, capabilities, and often times, at the poorly staffed affiliations, put in charge of a ward. I began to feel important, not bad. I desperately needed this space and the self-confidence it gave me.

The shamed little person slid into the past and all but vanished...or so I thought.

After I graduated, I enrolled in the graduate degree program. It was tuition free if I agreed to stay at Georgetown for two years and since my goal was to get my degree, this was a wonderful opportunity. I had already started classes when my father realized that since I would only be working part-time, I would not be donating sufficient income to the family and he demanded that I give up the degree program and move back home so I could work full time.

"We sacrificed so you could go to Georgetown, now you want to go back to school for another degree? How will it look if you are living in your own apartment in DC while I still owe people money?"

I did not honestly see the connection. I would still be giving the family money, just not as much. With a degree, I could contribute even more.

His demands made me feel selfish...depriving the family of income they needed after they had put me through school.

That old, uneasy, uncertain feeling came back.

On the outer level of things I tried at first to stand up for myself. I tried to rationalize with them that if I had a degree,

I could earn far more, but a voice inside was already weakening my resolve. It said, "Their needs are more important than mine."

Inwardly, I was undone before I started. Unbeknownst to me, a deep-level strata of belief had settled into place by all the years of finger-pointing, guilt, and shaming. And from that deep level, like an old, dark and powerful echo, a voice spoke whenever I thought of myself, did for myself, or tried to stand up for myself. The voice said, "I don't matter. I am not worth it."

I couldn't know it at the time, but this deep level "programming" would wreak terrible havoc later on.

I had developed a pattern of behavior that would one day nearly cost me my life.

And so, feeling that I was someone else's property to be dispensed at will, I accepted my father's irrational thinking, and moved back home. Inwardly, I harbored a feeling that I had betrayed myself by not standing up for what I wanted to do, and torn by the guilt of betraying my family, if I did not.

The three years I lived back at home allowed my father to stabilize financially, but I was not happy living in the old restrictive atmosphere. The saving grace was that I was happy working in the OR at the local County Hospital, partly because Georgetown sent their Medical students, Interns, and Residents there, and partly because of the wonderful friends I made in that close knit environment.

And so, another coil of habit settled into place around me: accommodation. I found ways to be happy in the bad situation I had agreed to be in. This distracted me from myself and the basic fact that I did not want to be living at home at all, giving my money to support the family.

I did become engaged, briefly, to the wrong man who

said the right things, but had the wisdom to become unengaged before we married. I liked his family and we got along quite well, but I think I saw him as a way out. We parted without tears, but I was a little depressed, because it was a disappointment.

Another piece of my inner pattern was emerging, which I could not see, of course and it was this: I was starved for the affection and approval I wanted from my parents. In my work, from our neighbors, and from the family friends, this need was more than fulfilled, but a basic need had been long neglected. I wanted to be connected in a positive way to someone exclusively who approved of me for who I was, not for what I could do for them. I needed to hear kind words, supportive words, and genuine affection. I was looking for this in the stability of a long-term monogamous relationship.

It is well known in psychiatric circles that we attempt to resolve in future relationships, the unresolved issues in our family of origin. I was attempting to fulfill this need in someone new.

By summer of '55 I was getting restless and needed a change. Fortunately, the family's financial situation was improving and I decided to move away from the area.

CHAPTER 3

PHILADELPHIA 1955

I REMEMBERED the numerous offers I had from a newly accredited hospital in Philadelphia and decided to look into the possibility of moving there. Eileen and Mike were ten and seven now and Johnny and Tommy, fourteen and thirteen. Mary Lou was married, Joan was working and Doris was in Nurses training at St. Joseph's in Baltimore. I felt comfortable leaving, so I accepted the offer.

I had made close friends the years I worked in the OR and they were surprised when I told them I was considering moving away. When I mentioned to them that I was going to Philadelphia to check out my new job, Harryet, my OR supervisor, and Khalil, a surgical resident who had been a wonderful friend from my student days, drove up with me. They were very impressed with the small private hospital and the beautiful grounds, but horrified at my living quarters. The place was in the process of being converted from a private estate to a hospital and what once had been a barn was now a temporary residence for the staff.

My room was small but bright and cheerful because of the large window that overlooked the beautiful grounds. A big square table that would serve as desk and dresser sat in one corner and someone had placed a vase of flowers on the middle of it. The bed looked as comfortable as the upholstered chair. I could put a small area rug on the floor later to make it more comfy and the single closet was large enough for the few clothes I owned. It was the first time in my life that I had a room of my own and I loved it. I would be very happy here.

Since I would no longer be sending money home, and both room and board were provided, I could now put away sufficient funds to return to school and finally get my degree. The professionals that shared the house with me were wonderful and I felt like I had a new family. Rose, who ran the lab, Janet, the nurse anesthetist, Maria, an OR nurse, and myself lived here in this renovated space.

Michael was the only Resident physician there and he had his own quarters in the hospital for convenience sake. He was right off the boat from Ireland and we had a lot in common as we were both the oldest of a large family. Michael was quiet, a lot of fun and a very good friend, but more like a brother than a prospective date.

It was September and school had already started so I would wait until next semester to enroll in one of the local colleges and at least get started on my degree.

In the meantime I enjoyed my new family and exploring the area with them. If I was happy at Georgetown, I was even happier here. I had my own space, even if it was only a room, but it was my castle. I had discovered my need for

A WAY OUT

independence, and I would never go back to being controlled again.

My new friends introduced me to Danny and not to offend them, I went out once or twice with him but found I was not interested. I was still dealing with another man problem that had followed me from Virginia.

Leo was a good friend of the family whom I had known from back home. He had asked me to marry him once before, and now, had come up to Philadelphia once again hoping to change my mind. He was a wonderful person, but a bit older, a widower with three children, and my family was pushing the marriage. I was not in love with him and not ready to be an instant mother. While I respected and liked him, I did not want to marry someone I did not love and I wanted to do much more with my life before settling down. I felt badly about refusing him, but felt even worse giving him false hope, so I told him I felt certain he would find the right person soon.

Leo might have been the answer to my needs, and I seemed to be the answer to his, but something important was missing. Despite his persistence and my family's pushing, I did not cave in under this pressure. Why couldn't I do this with my own family? Had I been so programmed that a part of me was unable to function when around them.

I now had said "No" to two men who wanted to marry me. Neither had ever tried to dominate me as my father had, both were spiritual, successful, attractive and good men. I had no trouble standing up for myself and making my own decisions when it came to them.

In the meantime, I was content being with my new friends and our trips to Kelly's Irish Pub across the road. We played the juke box, drank a beer or two, and once Michael even asked me to dance. Sometimes, Maria and I would drive up to

33

New Hope and walk around for hours. It was a quaint little village back then with lots of history, and it was fun. Rose, Janet I often did things together and they oriented me to the area which I began to call home. None of us had much money so our adventures were simple.

I would soon be looking into the local Colleges and did not have much time for romance anyway.

Several weeks after I arrived, my three housemates and I were sitting on the floor of Maria's room playing cards when Michael, the resident physician, stopped by to introduce a friend of his to the new nurse. Steve (I have changed his name for obvious reasons) was in his last year of residency at a large hospital in the City and had once worked here at our hospital. When the two men walked thru the open door, the other girls got up to greet Steve. They seemed happy to see him and asked how things were going and what brought him here this time of night. They were obviously quite fond of Michael's friend.

Steve was tall, olive skinned with short-cropped black hair and dark brown eyes that sparkled when he laughed. Even in his scrub suit, he was charming....I could not place where I had met him, but I felt that I knew him. So much about him was familiar; the way he spoke in low, strong, masculine tones, the way he moved, and the way I felt when he smiled at me. As fond as these people were of each other, I noticed that Steve pretty much ignored them, while centering his attention on me that night. It was eerie. I tried to think of where we could have met. At one point, he looked at me and said, "I know you from somewhere."

At various times during the evening he or I would think of someplace we may have met. When we could not find a single place where we both had been, we just gave up. He laughed and said it didn't matter, we'd figure it out one day. I could not shake the fact that everything about him was so familiar, even that laugh.

Only much later would I understand that his super-confidence, his personal power and dominant personality had hit a deep resonance at the core of my being—where I was both attracted to and a bit resistant to overly dominant males. This resistance was obscured by the fact that there was an immediate attraction to this man. *An attraction that I have never again felt in over fifty years.*

We finished the card game and the two men got ready to leave, but before they did, Steve said, "I'd like to come by and see you after work some evening. Is that OK?" We exchanged our schedules and he said he would like to come by tomorrow morning, since I was working evenings and did not have to be at work until noon.

The next morning he showed up as he said he would. He wanted me to see the stream that ran thru the property and the stone bridge that crossed it. We walked along the paths that wove through the property and soon came to the lovely stream. We sat on the cool stones of the little bridge and looked down at the water that flowed with great force under it. "Are you cold?" he asked, and put his arm around me. He drew me close and looking straight ahead, said he wanted to keep seeing me. As I turned to face him so I could answer him, he leaned down and kissed me. It was like no kiss I had ever felt before.

We slid down off the bridge and he took my hand as we walked along the tree-lined paths, kicking the fallen leaves out of our way. "Tell me about your family," he said, and then I asked him about his. He spoke of his deceased father, his mother, Molly, and his sisters. "You'd really like them," he said.

For the next three months I saw him every day except for the few days at Christmas when I went home to Virginia to visit the family.

In the evenings, he would come by the residence and we would listen to Montavani play....."Charmaine," "Greensleeves," "It Happened In Monterey," "Diane," and "Will You Remember." We listened to Edith Piaf, and to Liane, the sultry voiced damsel from Vienna. He knew the words to the German songs I brought with me, and I learned to sing, in German, one of our favorite songs; "So ein tag so wunderschoen wie heute," because I played it so often, but my favorite was still the romantic "Charmaine."

Driving into the city one evening, he reached over to hold my hand. "If I asked you to marry me, would you?" He said. "Yes." Then, "I want to marry you very much, but I need to get some issues in my life straightened out first." I was aware he had gone to Medical School in Germany after the war, and credentialing posed a problem in those days. "I don't care how long it takes," I said. He squeezed my hand tight and said, "I love you."

Soon after that evening, he asked me to promise him that I would never leave him, no matter what. By now, I was so in love with him, I couldn't imagine ever leaving him...and so I promised him that, "I will never leave you, no matter what."

A few mornings later, he came by the residence unexpectedly. I heard someone tapping on the window to my room from the outside and drew open the curtain. Steve was standing there, motioning for me to open the window. The door to the building was locked and he needed to talk to me.

I went down the hall and let him in. He kissed me hello and we walked down the hall to my room, because..."I need to talk to you in private, when no one is around," he said.

"There is no nice way to say this but please hear me out. I am married. I asked my wife for a divorce long before I met you but she refused so I did not pursue it and then when I met you, I approached her again." I pushed him away...."I love you, please don't push me away. Hear me out, please. We need to talk, please listen to me for a moment." He seemed to be visibly upset as he put his hands on my shoulders and looked into my eyes...

My hurt turned immediately to anger and I lashed out at him. Not a very effective response, but I could not help it. "How could you do this to me?" I was shaking and wanted to hit him, but could not. He took my hand and pulled me close to him. "I meant every word I ever said to you...I never loved another woman."

I was frozen in space. The ground beneath my feet was no longer firm, I was standing in a vacuum and beginning to come apart. My world was a blur like the words coming out of his mouth. I felt hurt, angry, betrayed, I was in a world of total disbelief. I could not even cry, and then I calmed down.

If he loved me as he said he did, then he was going through a difficult moment too. "Why didn't you tell me in the beginning?" I asked. "Because you would have walked away." And I would have. And I would never have known the ultimate joy of loving someone as I loved this man. All I could feel now was pain. Like no other pain I had ever felt, because I knew that now I *must* walk away from him. He was a married man.

At that moment I had no idea that he would live with his own pain for many years, and that I had indeed, inflicted it upon him. Nor did I realize that my loss at this moment was heralding an even greater loss.

In a matter of weeks, things became complicated. I was pregnant. It would have been easy to abort, but I refused to have an abortion and told him I was going to keep the baby. If I could not have him, I would at least have our child. I decided also, not to tell my parents until the baby was born.

He had been offered a position in another state when he finished his residency and begged me to go with him. I could have the baby there and he would be with me. Then his wife would have to agree to the divorce. I would have gone with him, if there had not been children involved, but there were.

The Chief of Obstetrics at our small hospital was my doctor and when I told him of my situation, he suggested adoption. I told him that was not an option. He then suggested I move into the City where I could be anonymous. He put me in touch with a private hospital and a position in the OR where I worked until the baby was born.

The pregnancy was uneventful until the middle of my seventh month when I developed signs of toxemia.

I had excess protein in my urine and my vision was blurred. I also had signs of liver involvement, and had gained 50 lbs. By the eighth month my blood pressure was over 200, all signs of severe toxemia. The diuretics I was given to lower the blood pressure were depleting my potassium and the leg cramps were painful because of it. I was short of breath and that, combined with the heat of summer, forced me to stop walking to work and to take the bus. The doctor told me to get off my feet but I continued to work because I needed the money to pay the rent.

A few weeks before my scheduled appointment, he called me into his office and very kindly, but firmly told me I had to let someone in the family know I was pregnant or make arrangements for adoption.

"I do not want to have to tell a mother that her daughter died in childbirth when she did not even know her daughter was pregnant." he said. The words that I might die were unbelievable, but all I could think of was what would happen to my baby.

I hardly heard the words: "You have less than a fifty percent chance of living unless we get the baby out and it is too soon." I desperately needed to look into adoption. The thought of giving up my baby was unconscionable and heartbreaking, but the thought of having my child moved from one foster home to the other was worse. I needed to know that my baby would be safe and loved in a caring home.

For days and days I debated and prayed, and since I knew my family would reject the child and no one was in a position to care for it, I tearfully, agreed to a private adoption which the doctor arranged.

I prayed all day and up to the moment I walked into the lawyer's office. The lawyer who handled the adoption was a short, stocky man who pompously sat behind his desk and motioned for me to sit. He made me feel like a criminal. He gave me some papers to sign, read me the rights of the *adoptive parents* and threatened me with court if I ever attempted to locate THIS child. THIS child was still MY child and this experience was not only extremely painful, but humiliating and I wanted to get out of this ugly, filthy place right then.

But he wasn't finished. "Come over here," he said, motioning with his hand. I stood up and walked over to his desk when he put his hand out. I did not even want to touch it but tried to be respectful, hoping the ordeal was over. He looked me in the eye and said; "You were very naughty and should be ashamed of yourself." As though I were a small child who needed to be reprimanded. I wanted to smack his ugly face and could not wait to tell my doctor what a piece of trash *he* was.

Before I could respond, he stood up, came around his

desk and smacked my backside. "You can go now, and in the future, behave yourself."

It was the ultimate humiliation.

Someone else might have walked out or really, slapped his face. How dare a lawyer, a professional, judge someone, anyone? But the word "shame" hit me deep in my soul, like a wrecking ball. Not only had I done something bad, I now was a morally defective being.

His words crashed through all the hard work I'd done to free myself of the old coils of guilt and shame laid in place by my parents, and to some extent, the Church. It brought back to life the old sentences that had grown weak and almost lost their hold: "How dare you?" "Who do you think you are?" "You're selfish, only thinking about yourself." "Don't you question me." "Oh, walk right and do something with your hair, and take those glasses off, you look like an old maid." The words of disapproval from the past were heaped upon his and I wanted to run somewhere, anywhere and be swallowed up.

But I walked out of his fancy office and out of the fancy office building like the proper lady I was not, and got on a bus to go home.

I was no longer acceptable in the eyes of my peers, my family, my Catholic friends or God.

When I left the lawyer's office that day I was mentally, emotionally, physically shaken. I had just signed papers that gave away a child that I wanted with all my heart. And on top of that, someone, a supposed moral authority had kicked me hard in the center of my being. I walked out bearing the one-word brand on my soul: *shame*. That one word followed me everywhere.

For days and weeks, shame tortured me. It was a deep

sense far worse than guilt and because the burden of carrying them both was too much, I buried them. I buried then deep inside me by telling myself that I had done what was right by caring more for my child than I did for my own feelings when I relinquished her to adoption.

I was too emotionally upset over the adoption to even consider telling my family, let alone listen to their own tirades, so I confided in a close relative who lived in Reading, Pa. She "knew" my family would not turn their back on me and would be helpful. I knew the opposite would be true.

Shortly after the announcement and their initial reaction, my parents notified me they were coming to Philadelphia to talk to me. What was there to say. The visit was a nightmare. I could not believe that a parent could be as cruel as my father was to me. My mother as usual, sat and said nothing. "How could you do this to us? You have disgraced us. I forbid you to ever mention this to anyone and you are no longer welcome in our house."

Thankfully, I had already made adoption plans when my father demanded that I have this child adopted. If death was not staring me in the face, I would not even be having that conversation. I told God I wanted to die that moment, but wanted my baby to live so asked God to forgive me and allow me to live until it was born.

Their visit lasted less than an hour but it seemed like an eternity. I was made to feel the shame I deserved. What hurt the most was the absence of compassion or caring from them that left me totally drained that day. I actually had expected them to be different at a time like this.

To save money, I walked to work in the inner city where I was living and continued to work longer than I should have. I was an OR nurse and the staff were very understanding so did not assign me to the long cases, but I still was required to be 'on call ' some nights.

For years, whenever I heard the loud sound of a jackknife drilling, it would immediately propel me back to that inner city hospital and the heat and the noise that kept me awake during those nights 'on call'.

After my parents visit, my sister, Joan quit her job in Va. and came up to stay with me until I delivered. She quickly found a job and this enabled me to stop working for at least 10 days before I delivered. My obstetrician decided to induce delivery early because of the toxemia, and when the date was set, my mother came up. I actually felt sorry for her. This must be difficult for her since she was under my father's rule and when she told me she had to abide by what he said, I thought to myself, "No you don't, you have a right to do what you feel is right," but I said nothing.

My condition continued to be unstable even after delivery, so I remained in the hospital for almost two weeks, every day praying that I would die now that the baby was safe. I felt I had nothing to live for. I felt I had lost everything I ever wanted.

My blood pressure finally came down sufficiently so I could be discharged, and once my family realized how sick I was, they allowed me to come home to recover. My good friends, Khalil and Claire drove me to the airport. On the flight home, I was pre-occupied with the dreaded, but inevitable confrontation, but was so deeply depressed over my double loss that I did not care what they would say. I would be glad to see my younger siblings and they would be my comfort, except there was no comfort on earth to relieve my pain.

A few days later, my mother suggested I visit Fr. Rush, the long time family friend. "He is concerned about you and

I think you should go see him. He wants to help you get through this."

I went to see him to keep peace, but doubted he could do much to help. When my secret became news, he suggested that I immediately go into a home for unwed mothers. A suggestion I rejected. He was a Theologian, what did he know about life.

I was interested in how he was going to help me, but since I had known him all my life and liked the man, I went. After greeting me, he walked across the room and pulled down the shade on one of the tall windows in the room. "That is what you must do. Forget the whole incident, block it out, it is past; act as though it never happened. The love affair, the baby, the adoption, forget it and get on with your life. You know this has devastated your parents, but they'll be all right." I thanked him and when I got up to leave, he asked me if I wanted to go to Confession. I thanked him and told him I had already been.

Walking back to my car, I thought of how many times I had been in this Monastery.

How many friends once resided here, how often my parents would go to one of them for advice or direction and I realized how little some of them knew of real life.

Did he care how I felt? How I was feeling? After all, I almost died. Did he give me any tools to feel better about myself? Did he know what loss felt like? He seemed to know how my parents felt. He was well aware of the trauma I had inflicted on them. Thank God some of these highly intellectual Men of God are not pastoral counselors, but he was trying to help. I may have been depressed, but I had the good sense not to take his advice the second time. He knew very little about psychology, emotions, reality, but he was a good Catholic priest and my family relied on him. This wasted trip at least got me out of the house for a bit.

The weeks at home dragged on with an unpleasantness that was stifling, I needed to go back to work but not around there.

I returned to Philadelphia for my six-week check up with the OB. He was pleased with my progress and glad to see the blood pressure coming down. He told me the baby was doing well and thriving and that it had saved a marriage. He told me that in all his years of practice he had never seen a patient as close to death as I had been who did not die. "' You are very lucky. "He then advised me not to get pregnant for at least five years because of the possible residual effects of the toxemia. I thanked him for all he had done and left. *I was lucky?* More wasted words.

I began to feel there was no one I could talk to. Who else could I tell this awful secret to who might understand. It was a forbidden topic within the family and I never knew if the younger siblings were ever told. I could not tell my classmates and certainly not my friends. There was no one, so I carried not only my secret, but my shame, alone, never speaking of it to anyone except my future husband before I married him.

CHAPTER 4

WHEN I RETURNED to Philadelphia for my post partum check-up, I stayed with my friend, Claire for a few days. She had been a good friend not only during the pregnancy, but after the baby was born. She came to see me in the hospital and when I was discharged, she and my old friend, Khalil, drove me to the airport to fly back to Virginia.

She mentioned that in my absence, the hospital had come a long way and the lovely new residence was finally finished. "Why don't you consider coming back here, they are looking for nurses and you would have a lovely suite of rooms?" I gave serious thought to the possibility because the atmosphere at home was smothering me. My parents continued to wail about what I had done to them and while I was forbidden to talk about it, my mother did not seem to be bound by the same rules. If I was going to heal, I needed to get away from the one place that should have been my comfort and refuge.

My primary concern was to leave home, and since I had no money at this time the hospital was a haven and a place to start over. However, it did present a very difficult situation for me and I needed to make sure I could handle it. The two people I most loved in the world...and had *lost*...were nearby. Could I deal with it? I knew it would be painful, but I had to confront the reality of my life and live with the consequences of the choices I had made.

The hospital re-hired me and I moved into my new quarters. My friend, Khalil was now a Resident at this same hospital he drove me to one year ago. The effects of parents' shaming had gone this deep; I expected everyone to despise and abandon me. Khalil, however, was even more protective than usual.

I had not seen or talked to Steve since he visited me in the hospital right after the baby was born. Because he was a physician, he was allowed to see the baby, but I had not been. My OB was adamant about this. "It will be easier for you if you never see the baby or know its sex." Later I would think what they really meant was it would be risky for me to see my baby, in that, once I saw it I might change my mind and once I knew its sex it might be easier to find it later.

Unbeknownst to all of them, the Pediatrician who checked the newborns came into my room the day after the baby was born and not realizing the baby was to be adopted, told me I had a beautiful little girl with lots of hair and was she perfectly healthy. She weighed 6 pounds, 5 ounces. This was all I had to remember her, and I clung to these sparse facts, holding them deep in my heart.

But the fact was, I now felt deeply alone in the world without the support of parents, shamed, and lacking any sense of dignity.

Once Steve found out I had returned to Philadelphia he called me several times and begged to see me. "Just for a while, please. We should talk." I was too emotional to even talk to him and finally told him that I simply could not ever see him. I might have been more adult and met with him, but it was just too painful. That, and I was too afraid of my own reaction to seeing him again. The one thing that helped me with this difficult decision was that since I had given up our child, I could not go back to him. He needed to get his own life in order. Eventually, he stopped calling.

And so I settled in as best I could and made a few superficial friends. Most of the employees I knew before were gone. Rose was the only one I knew who was still there.

It was two months since I'd delivered the baby, and now I needed to concentrate on losing the excess weight. Even though people said I looked great, I felt fat, never having weighed more than 100 pounds, I was now 120 pounds. Khalil said I always looked like a scarecrow so not to lose any more. He was an excellent surgeon and a well educated man, the kind of friend you could always count on, but very outspoken. He never minced words with me and I took the criticism well because I knew what ever he said was for my own good.

One day, back when we both were living in Virginia, he picked me up to go to a function at Georgetown. "That is a nice dress, but you need something more sophisticated." Another time, he found out I had met some friends at the local beer garden. "For God's sake, stop going there and go to...and he named a much more expensive restaurant. Khalil came from a wealthy family in Baghdad, and did not understand that I could not afford his taste. "Why did you buy that stupid little Ford?" he said one day. "Because it was all I could afford."

Those of us who knew him, let his comments roll off

because he said it as he saw it. I found his honesty, tactless as it might have been, refreshing and I loved him for it.

This day, however, he said something I did not want to hear.

"You need to get out of here. It is not healthy for you to be so close to your pain, and you will never meet anyone that is good enough for you around here. Go back to the DC area." "Khalil, I need to confront my pain, not run away from it," I said. "You're stupid," he said bluntly, and walked away.

"And you are stupid, too," I called after him, furious. "What are you doing here as a resident when you should be teaching in a prestigious University?" I shouted at his back as he retreated down the hall. How dare he walk away from me? I was not through yet.

"And besides, I do not want to meet anyone! How could I ever love someone else? I can't imagine loving another man... not for a long time. And I am *not* going back to DC."

He turned suddenly on his heel and came toward me. "I have never heard you even raise your voice, but now you *scream* at me? You have no idea how fragile you are right now." He put his arms around me and hugged me tight, not letting go...until I stopped crying.

He was right, he had only been concerned for me, more concerned for me than I was for myself. He had tried to break through the inner layer of self-punishment I was putting myself through by being here. No wonder he was frustrated. From a health perspective, by anyone's standard, what I was doing did not make sense. Self-abuse never makes sense—not to anyone but the one who is punishing themself.

It was now early October and one day I received a phone call from my best friend, Jeanne, in Virginia. She was getting married and wanted me to be her maid of honor. The engagement party was to be held at the Place Vendome, one of the finest restaurants in DC. in those days. Jeanne's fiancé, Marc, was the Maitre'd, and his brother, Blaise, who owned the restaurant, was to be the Best Man. I only had one month to lose this weight and find something to wear. The Place Vendome held many happy memories because Jeanne and I used too eat there quite often, sometimes twice a week...and on the house.

The engagement party and the upcoming wedding became rays of sunshine in my life right now and something for me to look forward to. It was just the distraction from my troubles that I needed. It was also a chance for me to look and feel good about myself again.

The weekend of the party, I drove down, stayed at my parent's house at night, but spent the rest of the time at Jeanne's with her family. We had a lot to talk about...the wedding plans, my world, and her whirlwind romance with Marc. It was good to have Jeanne to talk to, as she was the only friend I had told when I was pregnant and she had kept my secret. She had even come to Philadelphia to visit me while I was pregnant.

"I thought you were dating Charlie," I said. "Next thing I know, you tell me you're marrying Marc. When did all this happen?" "Well," she sighed, "Charlie didn't ask me to marry him and Marc did. And I found I love Marc very much. I know he's the right man for me," she replied. "But," she added, "Charlie will be at the party tomorrow...and I've also invited him to the wedding."

This did not register as a big deal with me. Charlie was a man I had met four years before, when Jeanne brought him along to a movie we were going to. I remember him being a lot of fun that night but he was getting divorced and divorced men were not in my pool of eligible men.

He was the new surgical Resident on the floor where Jeanne was the head nurse, and a really neat guy, she said. He just retuned from Korea, where he headed a MASH unit, and was finishing up a surgical residency in his specialty. He was upset over the divorce so she brought him along to the movies that night to cheer him up.

It is strange how an event that seems inconsequential is the event that changes your life forever.

At the Engagement Party, Jeanne re-introduced me to Charlie. I did remember him. He and I exchanged a few words and then I excused myself and moved along to mingle with friends. A few moments later, I was speaking to someone when Blaise approached me in his suave, charming manner and said, "Where is your 'steenger,' Nancy, don't you want one?" "No thanks, Blaise, I don't drink them anymore." Charlie, who I realized was standing next to me, looked at me and said, "You drink stingers? That's a powerful after dinner drink!"

I found myself telling him about the first time Jeanne and I went to the Place Vendome where Blaise had invited us in appreciation for the excellent care he received from Jeanne following his chest surgery at Georgetown.

When Blaise asked us what we wanted to drink, I told him 'something mild." Then, in his deep, French accent, he said, "You must have a steenger." From then on every time Jeanne and I walked thru the door of the restaurant, you could hear Blaise snap his fingers to get the bartender's attention: "Two steengers, please, for the ladies!"

Charlie thought this was awful. Do you know how strong a stinger is? Blaise said it was mild, I told him, and believing that, and with the amount of excellent French food that we consumed, I do not recall ever feeling we had too much to drink.

The cocktails were winding down and dinner was about to be served. Jeanne asked me where I wanted to sit and Charlie said, "She can sit right here," so I joined him.

I found him interesting and sophisticated. He was reserved and had a caustic sense of humor, which I liked, and an infectious laugh that made others laugh along with him. All in all, I truly had a wonderful time and was too occupied for those few hours to think about Philadelphia.

What struck me was the fact that he seemed to care about me and attempted to be protective, just as Khalil was, but in a different way.

As the evening came to an end, Charlie walked me to my car and said he was looking forward to the wedding. "I'll see you next month," he said.

It was a beautiful wedding at Sacred Heart Church, followed by a true Italian reception at one of Washington's landmark hotels. Later, when Jeanne showed me the pictures of the wedding party, Charlie was in many of them. "How come?" I asked. "Well, he was beside you all day, even when the pictures were being taken. I guess the photographer thought he was your husband."

For some reason, that struck another chord.

Before we had left the reception, Charlie asked me when I was coming back to DC. "I'm not sure," I'd told him. "But the holidays are coming up and I may be home for a day or two then."

"I want to see you," he said, surprising me with his directness. "Can I call you?" My heart was still very much somewhere else —with Steve, I'm afraid. Even so, while I was far from ready for another romantic interest, I felt quite safe where Charlie was concerned. After all, my mind was set: I could not marry a divorced man, nor would I get romantically involved with one.

Jeanne had told me before her wedding that Charlie was very lonely after his divorce—but also that he was not interested in a serious relationship. "He just wants company," she'd said. That was fine with me. Maybe I could use some company myself.

"Why don't you let me get in touch with you when I'm home," I replied, cautiously. I was not sure if I would contact him or not. He then asked if he could have my phone number in Philly. I hesitated, but did not want to seem rude, so gave it to him. I thought to myself, "How can I see another man when I am still in love with someone else."

The week after the wedding, he called. "Nancy, I was wondering if you could meet me at the Warwick next Saturday in Philadelphia. I would like to have lunch with you on my way to Reading to see my children." Jeanne had told me he had two small children but he had not mentioned them to me before. "They were babies when I was drafted into the Korean War," he explained. "And when I got back we only lived together for a short time before my wife moved out and we eventually got divorced."

I was surprised when he mentioned Reading. Reading was my mother's hometown, and I knew it well. So there was another connection to him. Not only was he suffering the aftermath of a broken and painful relationship and had suffered the loss of his children as well, he now had ties to a familiar area. I agreed to meet him.

That was the first of several consecutive week-ends we saw each other. Either he came up to Philly or I went down to

Virginia, and I had the blessings of Khalil who knew Charlie from their days as Residents at Georgetown.

Charlie enjoyed the finer places to eat and money did not seem to be an issue with him. I noticed that he dressed impeccably, not just for parties but as way of life, it was his personal style. I never saw him that he was not dressed well, hat and all. I appreciated this in a man.

Charlie had received several Holiday invitations and mentioned that he wanted me to go with him. He was popular and had many friends, some due to the fact he was a partner in a group practice within his specialty. I sensed he felt more comfortable socially with a companion, because he had been married and all of his associates were married.

This arrangement also allowed me to feel socially acceptable...for the time being, at least.

Dating Charlie, going to fine restaurants, socializing with professional people — all of it had the effect of helping me forget the past a little, and it helped distract me from the shame and self-loathing. These people liked me. And Charlie seemed to like me quite a bit, judging by the constant and cordial attention he was showering me with.

But I had not told him anything about my past. And so I lived with the feeling that one day the shoe would drop — that my sordid past would be known and I would no longer be acceptable.

When I came home for Christmas that year I was depressed. Charlie's presence in my life had been a godsend for keeping my mind occupied but these week-end trips were becoming a hassle with my schedule at the hospital.

On top of that, I thought of the baby all the time and with Christmas, it got worse.

Charlie took me to lunch at The Carriage House in

Georgetown the day he was leaving for Johnstown to spend Christmas with his mother. We each had a martini, ordered lunch and he talked about his family in Johnstown. "I am coming back right after Christmas because I have surgery scheduled and would like for you to be here for New Year's. Can you get back down?" "I cannot have both Holidays off, I know that."

"Then quit," he said. "You can move back here, get a job in the OR at Providence Hospital and we can stop this running up and down the highway."

On one hand I naturally recoiled. We had only known each other a couple months, but had spent a lot of time together. On the other hand, in a way, I needed this relationship. I felt accepted. Also, I saw the relationship with Charlie as temporary. Plus, I was also having a hard time living so close to Steve. Yes, moving back to Virginia would have its plusses. Ultimately, I remembered Khalil's words—It would be good for me to move away from Philly. And here was my opportunity. And so I decided to move back—but not home.

I found a room near Providence Hospital and found working in the OR quite pleasant, as I worked with many of the same surgeons I had once worked with at Prince Georges' Hospital in Maryland.

Six months into my employment, the Nun in charge let me know that I had two choices. "You can stop dating a divorced man—the one who happens to be on our staff," she said, letting me know I was being "observed" "—or you can resign." I resigned.

Through one of Charlie's patients he heard about an opening as a Visiting Nurse with AT&T, and fortunately they offered me the position. This meant that I would have to find a more convenient place to live. I looked at affordable apartments, but they were not very nice. Charlie suggested that I move into the Virginian in Rosslyn where he lived.

"I don't think I can afford that place," I protested. "Yes, you can," he insisted, cutting me off, ignoring my concern. "And there is an efficiency apartment available right now. I told them to hold it for you." "But..." I began to protest.

He cut me off again. This time the tone in his voice did not sound like he was *suggesting*...it was much stronger than that. "I want you closer to me." Then, as if to buffer the commanding tone, he added, "I'll help you out if you need extra money."

And so, in a subtle but distinct way, a pattern was beginning—but I did not see it. I was used to doing what someone of authority told me to, especially when it seemed to be "for my own good." And so I obeyed his dictate.

What I also failed to see was the dangerous and potentially deadly trap I was walking into.

CHAPTER 5

LIVING CLOSER to Charlie did make it easier. He was right about that. The immediate benefit was companionship. Whereas, in Philly I'd felt alone and isolated, now I had an attentive friend nearby. On weekends we would often drive out into the northern Virginia countryside, to the small town of Purcellville, where Charlie played golf at a country club while I swam in the pool. Later, we would have dinner with friends of his who lived there, then drive home to my place. Soon, too, I began accompanying him to Reading when he visited his children, because he did not want to go alone.

On one of these trips, barely one year into the relationship, a surprise was in-store. We were browsing in an Amish shop outside of Reading, when I noticed Charlie looking at me with an intense look.

"What is it?" I asked. "Is something wrong?"

"Wrong?" he replied. "No, not at all. I was just thinking."

"What about?" I asked.

His intense look softened and a smile crossed his face. "...I think I want to get married again...no, I *know* I want to get married again."

Suddenly, he leaned forward and kissed me — quickly, so no one would notice.

Time had passed since the devastating love affair with Steve and the birth of my baby. The past was not fully behind me, but months had gone by and time was beginning to ease the pain, and I realized that Charlie's heartfelt words comforted me. Maybe I could love and be loved. Maybe I needed to be married, too. It might help to heal the wounds of the past even more, and I definitely wanted to start a family.

Later, when we talked about our feelings even more, Charlie said that, since we were both Catholic, he would try to get an annulment from his first marriage. That would clear the way. I found my heart opening again...opening to this wonderful, strong man, who wanted me as his wife.

We had been dating about a year when Charles took me to Johnstown to meet his family. His late father had been an orthopedic surgeon and a well-respected pillar of the community. But he had died when Charles — as I'd started to call him — was only nine, at the height of the Depression. His mother, with her source of income gone, became adept at investing the existing assets. She was forced to downsize considerably, but managed to live a frugal, but comfortable existence.

We stayed at her house that weekend and I slept in the room with her. She invited a few close friends and Charles' sister and her husband for drinks before dinner. I had worked all day, had ridden for four hours, and was tired, but had to make a good first impression. It was obvious I was being scrutinized and 'tactful' questions were asked, but I passed.

One thing I noticed impressed me a great deal. Charles focused adoring attention on his mother. That was a good sign, I thought. On the other hand she responded in a reserved aloof manner. I could see this was a family with strong dynamics — a family steeped in tradition, roles played well, and high expectations for all concerned. Louise was, indeed, the dowager mother and looked the part, but I liked her.

"Don't be afraid of her," Charles told me. "She's strong, but she doesn't bite." One thing was clear. This proper family would never accept me — not with my past. Suddenly I felt myself in an awkward position.

I was exhausted by the emotional turmoil I was concealing when we got back to Virginia that Sunday evening. I knew I needed to have a talk with him very soon, but not tonight. I knew we would be having dinner the next evening at his place — because I would be cooking it — and my concerns could wait until then.

After work the next day, I drove across town to the Virginian, started dinner and, after we sat down to have the drinks he made for the two of us, I told him I needed to talk to him about something.

"Charles, I can't marry you. It wouldn't be fair. There's something I never told you. When I was in Philadelphia I fell in love with a married man I did not know was married." I hesitated, not sure how he would react, "and I had his child."

His expression did not change, he just sat there, quietly looking at me and not saying anything. Before he could respond, I quickly added, "My OB arranged for a private adoption and I told the father, who is a physician, that I could not see him anymore. The relationship is over. I have no intention of ever seeing or being in contact with him again. But

I am still trying to deal with the aftermath of the adoption. Only my family knows about it, but if your family ever found out, I am afraid it would not sit well with them."

I did not care to share with him any of the particulars, but did want him to know it was not a casual thing. The details were not his business and were my private domain. Later, I might tell him more, but not now.

I was surprised at how quickly he answered. "Nancy, it does not matter, and as far as my family is concerned—well, if and when they do find out, they will be so in love with you by then it won't matter." I felt relived. I knew that if I ever did marry, the man would have to accept this part of my life, and if he could not, then he would not be the right one for me.

"No one knows about this but your family?" he said. "No one but Jeanne."

"Good, and no one needs to know, either. We will never bring this up again."

Charles made us another drink, sat back down on the couch beside me, asked if dinner would be ready soon and said he was going to push the annulment.

I knew him well enough by now to know that he was strong-willed. He wanted to marry me, and he would have his way. He lost his two children to divorce and must know how hard it is to be separated from them, we would be on common ground in a sense, and I felt this could be a good relationship.

What I wanted most at this moment, though, was for him to hold me in his arms, tell me it would be OK and understand how I must be feeling about the loss of the baby. Instead, he said I needed to forget the past and he never wanted me to mention the baby again.

We decided not to discuss marriage with either family at this point. This was a good decision for me. In fact, I was still not *sure* I was in love with him and wanted to *be* sure before making a commitment. We would have plenty of time while waiting for the annulment.

And so we continued to attend social gatherings together, visiting his family, taking trips to the Jersey Shore, and going out to dinner. When his family knew we were traveling some place together, Louise would accompany us and she and I would share a room.

It took me several visits to feel her out, but I found I liked her and was not at all afraid of her as I think Charles was.

Later, I would realize I was missing important cues. Charles mother controlled him, her youngest child, by holding the purse strings tight, even while he was in Medical school. And she withheld affection. Control was the emotional game going on this family.

Nonetheless, Louise was good to me. Once, when I pulled my money out to pay for room service, she said, "Put your money away, Duchess," and the name stuck. I did not care about her money so had no need to placate her, and never had a problem being up front with her. Eventually, she and I developed a mutually respectable and fond relationship. I was the one sitting beside her bed when she died six months after we were married.

I had no idea then, of course, that in times to come Charles would attempt to resolve through me the unresolved issues he had with his mother.

Charles came from money and was making good money. I had neither and I have never been obsessed over it. My childhood was a continuous war over money and there was no way I was going to live like that. I knew how to save it, spend it and it did not matter if I had a fortune, as long as I had sufficient to survive...

During the next three years, I was introduced to a finer way of life than I had known growing up. My parents did not have a lot of money, but both came from good families and were educated. At home we were taught impeccable manners and would be sent away from the table if we did not use them. We said Grace before meals, which Charles' family did not. I did not know the pattern of the silver we used at home but was familiar with the lovely Irish linens my mother used at table. I called them "loafers," they called them "Weejuns." It became apparent to me that I was going to have a difficult time learning the names of things that lots of money could buy.

On the upside, I instinctively knew the basics of refinement and I learned quickly. I was careful to observe and soon developed my own taste for the finer things of life. If Charles and I married, I would want to be a proper wife and have him be proud of me.

Life those days was good. We knew the same people, spoke the same language, his family was more than cordial and made me feel a part of them and I loved my new job which allowed me freedom to meet him for lunch occasionally. I had respectability and as long as I kept my horrible secret, no one would know that I was not the wonderful person they thought I was. I knew I was acceptable and the compliments were real, but I felt deceitful.

While his family embraced me, my parents retreated into their former role. Once they found out Charles was divorced, I was not allowed to bring him into their home. So, I stopped going home. I now had two strikes against me. I also stopped allowing their narrow mindedness to have any impact on any of my future decisions, and I no longer cared if I pleased them or not.

The annulment was going nowhere and while I was getting discouraged, it gave me time to reflect on my feelings regarding Charles. Having experienced the pleasures of the forbidden fruit, I missed it as I was sure Charles did, so it was not long before we became intimate. However, I found little passion in our relationship, even two years later. Release, yes, but no passion. I chalked this up to the fact that he was so proper, he was waiting for marriage to display his skills.

The other matter that concerned me was that I did not feel the intense longing for him that I had felt for Steve. I missed him when he was gone, but did not feel as empty, and I wanted to love Charles the way I loved Steve, but did not. I rationalized that maybe we are only meant to have one great love in our life and are not able to love that way again.

I now know with all my heart that that is not so, you can love again and it can even be greater than the "one great love", but fifty years ago, I accepted the fact that marriage could survive with a common interest, a caring spouse, and being comfortable with each other. I resigned myself to the fact that we did have those qualities. But the over whelming thought that stared me in the face was the fact that Charles accepted my past and still wanted to marry me. Who else would have me? I thought.

Only one time in the three years before marriage did I see a sign of things to come.

One day he asked me about my finances. Did I have any outstanding bills? I did, and he wanted to see them.

I made a decent salary but I was a nurse and one rarely sees a millionaire nurse. I needed to dress better than I had in the past since we visited his family often and I spent more than I normally would have. My rent was much higher than any place I had lived before and I would *never* ask him for money. I paid my bills on time but not the entire balance.

When he saw that I had unpaid bills, he went berserk. I may have over–reacted to his raised voice and condemning words, but in a single instant, I was standing in the living room at home, my father screaming at me, accusing me of something that I did not believe warranted the attack, and I froze. Unable to respond to what was being said, I wanted to lash out at him!...tell him that these bills were the result of my trying to live up to a standard that I could not afford but that he expected of me., but could not utter a word.

I stood there listening to him with one side of my brain telling me to yell back at him...tell him you will not be spoken to in this manner, while the other side said, "You are not going to marry this man. Move out of this apartment and get away from him or your life will be a mirror of your childhood, but I was frozen and could not answer him...His words were trailing off, for in the back of my mind, I was seeing myself as the marked woman, I had broken a rule of society, my family had disowned me, the Church was about to, I had spent more than I made and the reason did not matter, I had done all of these things, and I could not stand to be screamed at. I hated this man right now and was never going to marry him.

"Where do you get the idea that you can spend more than you make?" he screamed. I reached for the papers that I had willingly given to him under the assumption he simply wanted to know my financial picture, but he grabbed them from me. I planned to have everything paid off before we got married and could have, but said nothing.

At that moment, I should have yelled right back at him and used the words that were going thru my head, but I could not. All I said was that he expected me to dress properly for the functions we attended and clothes cost money. "What about the dresses I bought for you at Dorothy Steads?" They were lovely and expensive but were formal and not something I would wear in the daytime.

Something had triggered this behavior in him and I did not know what it was. What I did know was that his outburst triggered something in me that made me very uncomfortable. I wanted to get away from him immediately.

He said he was going to pay off every bill and I was not to ever do this again. "Give them to me, I will pay them off myself. You are not my husband and I do not need you to pay off my bills." He refused and I told him I was going home and walked out the door. I decided I did not want to see him for a while. Who could I talk to about all this? No one. I refused to answer the phone the next day so he just came to my apartment and let himself in as though nothing had happened. I learned to do the same. It was not worth another scene by bringing it up again. A major mistake, and one I would make over and over and over until I learned to speak up for myself... but that was years away.

I believed that he realized he had gone too far and never spoke to me like that again. It was so unlike him that I never dreamt he was a volcano waiting to erupt. After that one incident, our lives returned to normal but I never forgot it.

By the third year, we both had accepted the improbability of an annulment, and I was beginning to feel that life was just too comfortable for Charles to change the status quo. I wanted to be married and start a family. He did not "want to be pushed; what's wrong with things the way they are?" "If you do not want to get married, just say so, but then I will start to date other men. I do not want to "be somebody's girl friend the rest of my life. I want a respectable life with a husband and a family."

64

Shortly after that, he told me to call my friend, Dan, who had a law practice in Philadelphia and ask him to find a judge that would marry us. We would go to Philadelphia and be married at City Hall. Then he said," We'll get married but I'm not having a house full of kids like your mother and sister."

The next week-end we drove to Johnstown to tell his family. Knowing none of them would attend any way, he thought it would be the decent thing to at least tell them. Since the date was not set, it made it easier. Such were the times of Church rule.

Friday passed and he had not said a word. We needed to leave early Sunday morning so that left Saturday. After breakfast Charles told me he and his brother in law were driving to Latrobe, pick up another brother-in-law and go to Ligonier to watch Arnie Palmer play golf. He thought it would be a good idea for me to tell his mother while they were gone, as she would take it better from me than him and he did not want to get into a hassle with her. "That's not fair! You tell her." "No, I want you to do it."

I did not build up to it, I simply told her we were going ahead without the annulment. "What are you going to do about the Church?" she said. I told her that I was not giving up my Religion, but hoped that when the Church saw we were already married, they may grant us the annulment and that the children would be raised Catholic, anyway.

She seemed resolved to the idea, then said," Why didn't Chad tell me this himself?" "Because he told *me* to tell you. He didn't want to get into a discussion with you over it."

The next morning she kissed us good-bye and I told her we would be fine and not to worry. She stood tall in the door way as we pulled out and I felt sorry for her. She was used to being in charge and this time, she could not call the shots but

I knew she would get used to it. Her religion was so important to her and I wondered it it were, why didn't they say grace before meals. *Such a dumb thing to be thinking.*

We were married June 28, 1960 at City Hall on the hottest day of the summer. Claire and Dan arranged for us to use their Country Club for the reception which included some of our friends from DC, some of Charles friends from his days at Jefferson who lived in the area and my sister, Joan, the only member of my family to attend.

We went to New York for our honeymoon and stayed at the Hotel Pierre for four days.

CHAPTER 6

WE RETURNED from New York to the four bedroom Colonial we purchased two months before we married. The next day, Charles' mother and her friend, whom the family called "Aunt Elene" were driven down and the four of us left for Stone Harbor, New Jersey for one week. We enjoyed the ocean and the beach, but I was anxious to return home and settle into married life.

Back at work that Monday, I felt quite happy and proud when I saw the sign on my desk: *Nancy Hannan, RN.* I felt as though I had arrived. I finally made it safely across the deep chasm that at one time threatened to swallow me up, dragging me down into unimaginable depths.

On the surface life was as it was supposed to be...and I thought that slowly, I would be able to move beyond the past and it would cease to be as painful...this is how others get through insurmountable grief, I thought; they replace it with something else.

The first week we were married, I noticed that when I would come home from work about six o'clock, the ladies who lived on either side of our house would be outside talking and immediately come over to talk to me. They were both lovely and very friendly.

Unless he was playing golf, Charles was often home before I was, but did not go out to visit. The second day, he called to me from the house to 'come on in.' "In a few minutes," I called back. He then came out, and in front of the ladies, told me to "Get to the kitchen, and start dinner." Thinking he was being funny, I tried to engage him in the conversation the three of us were having, but there was nothing funny about his response. "When you come home from work, you do not stand in the front yard talking, you go into the house where you belong, and get dinner." And with that, he headed for the house, turned back to me, and said, "Now." I followed him inside. *Big mistake.*

I wanted to defy him and finish our conversation, but instead, said something to the effect that "I had better go in, don't know what the hurry is, but there must be a reason." I was embarrassed, did not want to make a scene in front of the neighbors, and instead of apologizing for his rude behavior, I defended him.

Inside my head a very familiar scene had just played out. My father demanding that I return from wherever I was, or stop whatever I was doing to come at that moment.

The scene was overlapped by the feeling I was also dealing with a two year old sibling having a temper tantrum. In essence, that is exactly what I was dealing with. A controlling husband who was having a temper tantrum. And I responded as I had been programmed to.

I disregarded something else that struck a cord but only recognized it much later. On several occasions over the three years we dated, if I was engaged in a conversation with someone else, he would come over and want to know what we were talking about, and then draw me away from the conversation.

It was too early in the marriage for me to see the pattern that was evolving, and too late when I did figure it out.

Once inside, I made it clear that he had been rude. "We can have discussions in private, but not in front of neighbors," I said. "And why can't I visit for a few minutes with the two women who live on either side of us? We need to be polite to them, we may be living here for a long time."

He ignored what I had just said because he had something else to say. "And while we are on the subject, there is another thing. You do not get chummy with the neighbors...and no one comes into this house without my permission, and that includes your nurse classmates. And *I* will choose our friends in the future. Is that clear?"

All of a sudden, my classmates were not high enough on the social scale to come into my home? Jeanne was a classmate and he dated her. Our neighbors were professional people, including two physicians from Georgetown who lived down the end of our street.

He can't be serious, I am thinking. Where did all of this come from? We never ate dinner at six o'clock. I want to enjoy the summer evening, the people around us, our yard; this is our new life, why are we hiding from it? Is he afraid I will reveal our secrets? For he had one, too. I was told early on that I was never to mention that he had been married before and had children. *His* secret was not shameful, unless you considered divorce shameful, and maybe he did. I was dumbfounded and disturbed by his words.

But more than disturbed, it made me rebellious. I will not be controlled. He could at least have a normal discussion with me about his feelings and wishes. I was determined to defy him in such a way that he would not notice or at least get used to it. Rudeness is inexcusable. I *will* talk to my neighbors. And I did.

When I brought the subject up later, I asked him why he had not discussed his attitude with me before and why he felt this way...he was always so friendly. I got no answer. I decided that I was not going to obey a rule that did not make sense. To keep peace, I met my classmates somewhere else for lunch or dinner, chatted with the neighbors when he was not around, and made friends with the people of his choice.

Yes, the message was clear, I was not yet on his level, still not quite good enough. Then why did he marry me?

Years later, when a psychiatrist asked me if I could remember the first time I saw something different in him, I related the above incident. "How could you have known beforehand," he said. "Only an Obsessive Compulsive would be able to hide his true nature for three years. A leopard does not change his spots, only his tactics, until he catches his prey."

I did not know it at the time, but I was married to a controlling, obsessive compulsive who could not be easily changed. I needed all the help I could get but did not know how to ask for it without giving away the awful secret that needed to be kept buried...and without facing the shame I could not face.

Soon after, Louise's health took a downhill turn. She had been tired and short of breath at the Shore, but no one seemed to think too much was wrong. Once home it was discovered that she had severe anemia. Charles' brother, a Radiologist at the Cleveland Clinic, took her there for further studies and it was found that she had colon cancer. Following surgery, she seemed to do fairly well and returned to Johnstown. But her condition continued to deteriorate.

Our near weekly trips to Johnstown were taking their toll on Charles, and he was becoming difficult. His brother asked me to try and convince my husband that everything possible was being done for their mother, and he needed to accept the fact that she was dying. He could not. At one point Charles told the family he was bringing his mother down to our home where I would take care of her. This did not sit well with the rest of the family but she had the final say and told them that she wanted to stay at home.

Toward the end, I took one week off and I believe my presence was appreciated, as I would run various errands and sit with her at night so his sisters could go home. I also noticed that Charles was very emotional, a factor that he kept well hidden up until now.

One of the things I had admired about him was his strong self control, his calmness in a difficult situation, and his ability to keep a level head. He was the opposite here and I could see the family's reaction was not sympathetic. In fact, he clung to me and I saw a very different person than the one who told me to 'get to the kitchen.'

By now, six months into the marriage, I had more conflicting messages than I could handle. While I had begun to feel competent and accepted, the next message tossed me back into the heap of rejects. The day after the funeral, his mother's valuable jewelry was to be divided...the rest of her household items and furniture, later.

We gathered back at Louise's house and were standing in her lovely living room where the division of the jewelry was to take place. Charles' older sister turned to me and said, "You realize Nancy, that since you are not Charles' legitimate wife, you are not entitled to *any* of Mother's jewelry." I was taken back! What a callous thing to say at a time like this. I was already sad at losing this woman I had become close to, and now to be reminded that I wasn't a legitimate wife! Wasn't there a more decent way of letting me know ahead of time, so I would certainly not have been there. And where was my husband? I was hurt and disappointed in him that he said nothing, not to her or to me. He just stood there as though 'that was it'.

Once more, I felt devalued, and by my husband. As for my mother-in-laws' jewelry, I did not care about her jewelry, but I would loved to have had something personal of hers. The sense of having been devalued at this sad time hurt deeply. My husband, his family, and the Church...to all three, I was not deserving.

What I should have seen was how easily he deferred to the women in his family of origin. Accustomed to a domineering, controlling mother and two older sisters, he could not stand up to them.

I should have recognized that one day he would see me as an extension of his mother and/or sisters and I might exert the same control over him. To avoid this possibility, he would need to control me. He would treat me as he had been treated. *And he did.*

When her household furnishings were being divided among the four children, I was not involved, being the illegitimate wife, so I wasn't sure what we would end up with. Our new home was sparsely furnished with items from his first marriage and we could use some additional good furniture.

When I saw what was delivered the following month, I was a bit disappointed at first, but then realized that those black dressers and chests and tables that no one else wanted were probably beautiful underneath. Once the black stain was removed, we had valuable pieces. And who refinished all this furniture? The parents of our next-door neighbor who I was not supposed to talk to.

Following his mother's death, Charles became a little less reclusive with the neighbors, but always kept them at arms length. When we realized I was pregnant, he seemed delighted and was in a good mood most of the time, sharing the news with everyone, including the neighbors.

Our social life migrated to the people Charles wanted to associate with. I liked them and we got along well. I was happy being around people but was always cautious of what I said, and careful not to make reference to Philadelphia. Afraid that some little telltale something might slip, I found that I became less talkative, more quiet in crowds, and more sedate than usual.

We looked forward to the baby and Charles kept telling me he hoped for a little red headed girl. I refinished furniture (from his previous marriage) for the nursery and since I had stopped working after his mother's death, had ample time to prepare for the event. I felt good and while I had no pregnancy related problems...I often thought about my last pregnancy. It had been nearly five years now, but being pregnant brought it all back, and with it, the memories.

Still, Charles and I seemed happy and there were no more "money" issues. We entertained at home and his family visited quite often. I felt comfortable that life would continue like this and hopefully, for the rest of our lives.

The only disappointment was our sex life. Marriage had not improved it. I accepted this as punishment for breaking God's law, still, I felt cheated. Whenever I would attempt to discuss or make a comment in this area, he would always refer to my "old boyfriend". It was insensitive and so hurtful that I learned to keep quiet and accept things the way they were. I would have to find an acceptable outlet for this energy...

In the prime of my life, I gave up what should be a joyful bonding of two people.

I had learned well, how to accommodate, but there was also a price to pay. I found myself longing for the love, warmth and passion of the other man.

On Labor Day, we entertained some close friends for dinner. The baby was due the week before, so we lived minute by minute. After our guests left, I cleaned up the kitchen and went to bed, feeling tired, with only an occasional contraction. Remembering Charles' edict to be "sure you are in labor before waking me" I tossed and slept fitfully until I was sure. In fact, by the time I woke him, I was so sure that we barely made it to the hospital.

I recall wanting to wake him earlier when I first got uncomfortable, but I have a high threshold for pain, so did not realize how close I was, and certainly did not want to disturb his sleep. I see now that by not asking for help or comfort, I was setting a precedence.

Years down the road, I continued to believe that he would 'see' when I needed help, would understand my needs, would know I was in pain, either physical or emotional. But why should he, I never asked for help. I seemed to manage without it. Maybe if I had made a lot of noise, cried out with the first contraction, wakened him and asked him for help in the beginning, the future years would have been different.

I did not feel comfortable asking. I did not believe I deserved his comfort. Since I did not "deserve the maternity clothes" I once purchased, my subconscious mind, having been fed once more with the image of 'not worthy', I simply responded to it.

I wanted the finances to be in perfect shape before the baby was born, because I knew I would be very busy after I got home. I paid all the bills in full, and a few that would come due soon so Charles would not have anything to complain about.

After Cara was born, and seeing how busy I was with the new, colicky baby, he took over the checkbook. This was fine except I now had to ask for the money I needed for myself. In addition, I needed to justify everything. "What is that for, why do you need it, didn't you just buy some? etc. etc." I suggested he give me an allowance so we could end this ridiculous game..."You do not need an allowance," he said.

Money became an item of control, not a medium of exchange and all the sense in the world of this could not break down the barrier within me to not only ask for it, but to demand that I have an allowance. Over the years, I would approach the subject many times. His response was varied, but carried the same connotation. "You do not deserve it." *I more than deserved it, why couldn't I say this to him?*

My attempts to discuss money were futile. He always had a comeback and my responses never satisfied him, no matter how logical. He had a set pattern and repeated the same things over and over.

"Where would you be without me," "I bailed you out once before, and I am not bailing you out again." "Who do you think you are, that you can spend my money without my permission?" One time, he threw in a different comment: "If it weren't for me, you'd still be in the gutter." He only said that to me *once*, because this time, what he said had no truth to it and I reared back at him. "I was *never* in the gutter, I was a young woman who fell in love with the wrong man and I paid a heavy price for it. Don't you ever say that to me again." And he never did.

So often his comments were out of context for the situation, and I could not successfully argue with him. I felt trapped in this financial fiasco that seemed to me irrational and pathologic.

So, to avoid the unpleasantness of criticism and ridicule, I went along with the charade. Had I confronted him or threatened leaving, he may have relented, but I was not in a position to follow thru with my threats...and as the family grew, these monetary discourses became increasingly unpleasant. I no longer *felt* trapped, I *was* trapped.

And there seemed to be no possible way to extricate myself given the fact that I now had two small children and was determined that they were going to have the life I intended for them to have.

There was no place for me to go, and I had no access to money. I was staying in this marriage and would make the best of it. I would find a way to solve the money problem. We had two beautiful children and a lovely home and good friends. He'll get over his insecurity over money.

I had no way of knowing how much worse it would get.

Many years later and after a bitter battle which I won, he said to me," I would have given you the money if you had fought harder." "And things would be very different between us now, if you had treated me with respect and dignity instead of forcing me to beg for what was rightfully mine."

The feeling of 'not deserving' was so deeply imbedded in my belief system those earlier years, that I was unable to have fought harder. I expected my request to be honored as any normal husband would honor his wife' request, instead, I was made to feel like a servant.

I did not see that *my own* view of myself was reflected in how he saw me...not worthy.

CHAPTER 7

IN THE DAYS after my pregnancy test returned "positive" with the second child, Charles anger did not subside. Whenever his condemning words reached my ears, I would retreat into another world, a dark, unforgiving place where I could be invisible. His words parroted what I had heard before, and I regressed into that other person. His accusations triggered a response that prevented me from lashing back at him. All I was able to do was ask him to please stop. But he would not.

Instead, I worked hard to reassure him, make him feel better. I told him that I would be able to handle two babies. The new baby was not going to be a problem or his concern.

There was another issue for Charles. My pregnancy was embarrassing to him...his wife pregnant so soon after one baby. How could he ever tell his family..."They will be mortified," he said, over and over.

And so, for a whole winter, I was to stay inside. "I do not

want you parading around the neighborhood pregnant," he said to me one day. That familiar, sinking, uneasy feeling came over me and I found myself embarrassed to be seen in public. I went to Church by myself and waited until spring to take Cara for her walks.

When the warmer airs of April came, I was blossoming along with the flowers and the neighbors seemed very pleased to see another baby on the way. They made me feel good and I was happy.

The months that followed were a mixture of acceptance and displeasure. Always delighted with our daughter , he would flare up at the thought of another child and my hopes that he was accepting the new baby would diminish. Yet, there were times when we would actually be on normal terms.

Charles liked to eat in quality restaurants but it was difficult to find a competent baby sitter for Cara. I knew it was important to go places with my husband and I did enjoy eating out as well. But trying to find a sitter that he found competent was a hassle.

It was not unusual for him to come home and announce, "We're going out for dinner tomorrow night," and expect me to have an available sitter. I looked forward to these evenings out because we would have somewhat of a conversation and a lovely dinner. Securing a good sitter was high on my list those days and I finally found someone reliable.

The greatest difficulty was in convincing Charles that she was competent and the baby would be properly cared for. He would repeatedly ask me, "Are you positive she knows what she is doing?" As a mother, I certainly would not leave my infant in the hands of someone incompetent. I felt this third degree interrogation was more questioning my judgment and began to resent his interference. I told him that, but I now had a new angst to deal with...what if she *was not* as competent as I thought.

What I did not notice then was the way his anxiety began to spread from one small matter to another. And also the way I slowly became the caretaker of his emotional well being.

In the beginning, these minor anxiety attacks of his centered around the baby and then I noticed that money would elicit a similar response. When the subject of money came up it was never a normal discussion. It was an order, a demand, an accusation. I would say to him," You do not need to yell at me, you can ask, or tell me but it is not necessary to raise your voice in an accusing manner. Couples discuss these issues, you do not need to start out blaming me." His response was always the same. "You cannot continue to spend money, I just do not have it." That did not make sense to me because he did have it and I was far more frugal than he was. I shopped carefully and bought the best we could afford because it lasted longer, while he spent indiscriminately, for himself. I would shop for baby clothes and food for the family. He would buy golf clubs.

Ever so slowly, he tightened the controls on my spending anything. If and when I made a purchase it had to be with his approval. This meant that I did a lot of footwork before approaching him...not the best use of my time with small children.

Unsettling as Charles' anxiety and controlling nature were, it was the screaming that undid me. I would freeze inside, while appearing calm on the outside. Growing up, we were poor, but so was everyone else in the thirties and forties and it took money to raise a large family. My father worked hard, but not hard enough for my mother who was trying to feed and clothe eight children. At night, while in bed, I could hear their discussions over money that escalated into loud screaming. I could not stand it and felt guilty that we children cost so much. After hearing sufficient of these sessions, I vowed that I would never scream about money and my husband and I, when I did marry, would always have a normal discussion and never blame the children for any lack of money.

Charles and my father became one and the same...the yelling, always making me small, and selfish for spending money or not having enough.

I see now that the long-range effect of those childhood years was that I had not been able to separate myself from the reality. I had married my 'father' and was responding to Charles in the same way. I was unable to extricate myself from being the small child who cost so much and created the money problem, from the wife who spent her husband's money.

I realized early on that money was a big issue with Charles...but could not understand his anxiety over it since we had a comfortable income. It was my spending his money that seemed to trigger an outburst. I found that to keep peace, I would have to refrain from spending any money at all...an unnatural expectation.

We charged our groceries at Country Club Market and he never complained about the monthly statement which he paid. (By now he was paying all the bills.) I ordered whatever I wanted and the groceries would be delivered. I soon learned that I could tack on about $50/month for some discretionary spending money and he did not notice this at first.

I did not shop in a super market until the Country Club Market closed some years later, and then when I was forced to shop at Giant or Safeway, he scrutinized the bill and my source of spending money disappeared. I was to ask him for any cash I needed, and I "did not need an allowance."

I desperately needed to talk to someone about the demeaning treatment I was receiving.

Because we had been married out of the Church, I felt uncomfortable going to a priest. I was alienated from my family and from some of my friends, as well. I felt alone and abandoned. I certainly could not talk to the medical community...they were his livelihood and his image was crucial to his success. I had no one to confide in.

Still, I looked forward to the medical meeting we were planning to attend in Charleston, SC. that March. My greatest concern though, was what to wear. This would be my first meeting with this group of physicians and their wives, and I wanted to look my best.

Recalling an incident while pregnant with Cara relating to maternity clothes, I now had to figure out a way I could buy better looking clothes for this trip.

One day, before we were married, I remember Charles telling me about how nice his former wife looked when she was pregnant. It was during his residency at Gerogetown and they were living in the area. He told me her maternity clothes came from a specialty shop on Connecticut Avenue in Washington, DC.

I knew how important it was to Charles that I look well dressed, so I went into DC, found the specialty shop he spoke of and carefully picked out several maternity outfits. I felt certain he would be pleased with my choices as he had often bought me the kind of clothes he wanted me to wear, and these fell into the same category.

That evening at dinner, I told him I had found some nice,

classy maternity clothes and thought he would really like them. I felt great in them, trying them on. "I'll show them to you later."

That evening, we watched a little TV, chatted a bit and then he said," Let's see what you bought today."

I was so pleased with my purchases I couldn't wait for him to see them. I rushed upstairs, slipped into the first outfit, and smiled as I smoothed the skirt in front of the mirror. When I came downstairs, I felt great...even better when Charles nodded his approval.

"Where did you buy them?" he asked.

"In the Maternity Shop on Connecticut Ave. in DC. I remember your saying how much you liked the clothes in there, and thought you'd want me to go there, too.

Suddenly, his expression soured. *"Take them back! Tomorrow!"*

I was stunned. "Take them back? Why? You said you liked them! What's wrong with them? Why do I have to take them back?" *"Because you don't deserve them!"* he said, and he went back to the study.

The words hit me like a bolt from the heavens! Because I didn't *deserve* them. Why didn't I deserve them. I was pregnant with his child. He wanted, expected, demanded I look proper, and now he wants me to take back lovely clothes that should have made him proud of my appearance...he never even asked how much they cost, so it wasn't that...What in God's name was the problem.

His response simply reinforced the image of myself that I had so desperately attempted to alter.

The next day, my heart in ashes, I made the trip back into DC. and complied with his wishes. I hated him...but was unable to challenge him...so I obeyed him...the voice of authority. These same feelings would surface many times over the years...I did not know back then something I would find out years later.

When it came to spending money, the amount did not matter *if he* made the purchase.

His sister told me later that *he* had bought all of Charlotte's maternity clothes.

I was determined to have better-looking clothes for this trip than the ones I wore with Cara, so asked for money to buy some. "You do want me to look appropriate when meeting your colleagues, don't you? And if you don't want me to show, then I will need clothes that not only fit, but will hide the pregnancy."

Reluctantly, he gave me the credit card and I bought s few lovely maternity clothes...realizing I may never wear them again, but so what...I felt I did deserve them this time.

The drive down to Charleston with little Cara was rather tiring but I knew better than to complain. I had orders not to mention the pregnancy to any of the physicians' wives and hopefully, my clothing would not give me away. The trip was relatively pleasant and I found that when away from home, and if he could play golf, Charles could be a reasonably decent human being.

Once back home, I talked to God a lot. We 'd had three and one half happy, fun years before we married. What happened? Was I really being punished or had I missed the signals? I felt I had nowhere to turn, and resigned myself to living this kind of life...and no one need ever know.

Sometimes I wondered if God was listening. Maybe God

wouldn't listen to a defective, selfish person like me.

His family from Pennsylvania were frequent visitors to our home. I liked them and enjoyed the times we spent together, but now they were on his side and I believed that a husband should defer to his wife, but he did not. When they visited, I was often told to go to bed long before I was ready, because "you need your rest." I felt that it was so they could talk among themselves, which I could overhear them doing, once I was upstairs. His deference to his family, instead of to me was disturbing, and I realized that blood was truly thicker than water.

As the months went by he seemed to accept the status quo and was a bit quieter. The colicky baby got better and I no longer had to drive her around for hours at night so her father could sleep.

In July, the three of us went to the Jersey Shore. Again, it was a very pleasant time as Charles loved to show off his precious Cara. He would play with her on the sand and especially in the water, which she loved. This enabled me to swim in the ocean where my eight-month pregnant body felt buoyant and relaxed. Maybe all would be well after all. I hoped so. I was tired of keeping the peace at the expense of not being able to talk about issues I wanted to discuss...God forbid something might set him off.

I became intensely aware of other couples' interaction with each other, and noticed that many of our friends acted in a loving way, at least in public, even when displeased with the spouse. It was not uncommon to hear one of them say, "Well, I still love you, despite the fact that you...." But I had come to realize that Charles' love was conditional....If I upset him, he would not act loving toward me. If all was quiet and peaceful at home, he was pleasant. I needed recognition that I was important to him but never found it. I saw that he loved our little girl, and I could foresee the day when that love too, would be compromised once she did something to displease him.

The pregnancy was uneventful and I began to get things ready for the new baby. I was actually looking forward to him/her.

CHAPTER 8

AUGUST, 1962

I WENT INTO LABOR a few weeks early while at the hairdressers one Friday afternoon.

Rushing home, we called a local baby sitter to stay with Cara until the woman I hired could get there. On the way to Georgetown Hospital, Charles' anxiety level went off the chart. "Why would anyone in their right mind go into labor during rush hour?" he bellowed.

"Because it was not my idea and besides, you are going against the traffic, so just keep on driving," I replied.

He was unaware of how much I needed a bit of comfort, a word of encouragement, a simple, "You'll be fine, I'll be there with you." It did not occur to me at that time to ask for those words of comfort, because I still felt guilty for upsetting him by getting pregnant. It did not occur to him that he played a significant role in this!

All I could think of at the moment was the early morning when Cara was born less than one year ago. He had told me to be certain I was in labor before we called the doctor because it was humiliating for a physician to take his pregnant wife to the hospital in false labor. So, as I dutifully waited for the ten minute interval, the contractions came one on top of the other until I realized we needed to get to the hospital immediately. When we arrived, I was fully dilated and ready to deliver. There was no time for any regional anesthesia. It was not a pleasant delivery.

But now, instead of reassuring me, he reminded me that there had been two maternal deaths recently, at Fairfax. There were no comforting words for me, so I simply reassured *him* that I would be fine and he needed a little more faith. Less than one hour later, I heard the words that any mother would love to hear; "You have a beautiful baby boy."

My husband was nowhere in sight, but he did come into the recovery room. "Well, you've got your little boy, hope you're happy. I'm going home to check on Cara." No asking how I felt. Was he jealous? What kept him from being happy with our new baby.

His behavior confused me. I expected him to accept what he could not change and that hopefully, we would be able to resolve the deeper issues at a more opportune time.

Right now I had two babies to take care of.

A sudden thought crossed my mind, but I dismissed it : "Forget any help, you are on your own."

The next morning the head nurse came into my room, but without the baby. "Is there something wrong?", I asked her.

"Yes, your baby has an AB/O blood incompatibility and needs to be transfused...very soon." "This can't be, my husband is A+, that's on his Army dog tag." "Well, either the army made a mistake or he is not the baby's father." Then she laughed because she knew both of us.

"When you call Charlie, let him know what is going on and ask him to get his blood typed again. In any event, the baby needs the exchange transfusion as soon as possible."

Lying in bed, dealing with the possibility that my baby might die, I listened to the frantic ranting of my husband on the phone. Another crisis! "You are responsible for all this!"

Again, I tried to reassure him, all the while, needing reassurance myself.

HERE IS WHERE I MADE MY BIG MISTAKE. I WAS NOT REPONSIBLE FOR ALL THIS. HE WAS. I NOT ONLY ABSORBED THE BLAME, BUT FAILED TO CONFRONT HIM WITH THE REALITY THAT THE ARMY MADE A NEAR FATAL MISTAKE, AND HIS NEED FOR INSTANT GRATIFICATION RESULTED IN THE PREGNANCY. AND I NEEDED SOME COMFORT FROM HIM, A PHYSICIAN WHO WAS AWARE THESE BABIES CAN DIE FROM A BLOOD INCOMPATIBILITY.

Those thoughts were alive in my head and I knew them to be so, but I kept quiet.

Why?

My husband was re-typed and found to be AB+, but that did not calm him down, now he was imagining what would have happened if he had been wounded in Korea and given the wrong blood...He would be dead.

The neonatologist reassured me the baby would be fine, once transfused, and they planned to do it as soon as possible.

However, he would need to remain in the hospital for several more days for observation. Two days later, I was discharged but went home without the baby.

Five days later, when the hospital called to notify me that the baby was discharged and could be picked up anytime , I called Charles at his office to tell him.

"You had him, you go get him." And he hung up.

A short while later he called back and said he would take me the next day which was a Saturday.

When we arrived at the ER entrance where he could park in the doctors' parking area, he turned the motor off, and told me to go up and get "him." "You're not coming with me?" "No." So, I went alone to the business office, then up to the nursery where I picked up the baby, dressed him, wrapped him in his new blue blanket and, with the baby in my arms, got on the elevator, alone, and rode down to the main level.

I got off, walked down the familiar halls of my Alma Mater, thru the ER and out to the waiting car, carrying my newly transfused and beautiful little boy.

l wanted this to be a happy occasion. As I showed the baby to Cara who was in her car seat in the back, she grabbed his little hand and tried to pull him close to her. My husband turned the motor on and told me to "get in."

My heart felt like it weighed a ton. How can you make someone feel? I thought about growing up and as the oldest of eight, I remembered what it was like when a new baby was brought home from the hospital. It was a time to rejoice. My father was so proud, he would hold the baby, take it around to the younger children to look at and tell them to be careful, don't breathe on him/her. That is all I wanted now, for my husband to be proud of his child and hold him lovingly, but he would not even look at him.

That night, after I fed the baby I put him in his crib in the back bedroom where I had planned to sleep also, not sure if he would be colicky like his sister, and possibly disturb his father. I then put Cara to bed in her room next to the master bedroom.

I was telling her about her little brother and she was trying to say, 'baby'. Charles, who was in the next room, began to mock her and then raised his voice to me, filled with anger, animosity, and accusations. He let me know that "you had them, they are yours, don't expect any help from me. They are all yours," he said.

Even if he did not mean these words, I heard them and they had a very strong impact on me. That night, standing beside Cara's crib, the reality of my life became apparent. He has rejected his own children, if not in reality, in words, and he has devalued me. This is not acceptable, but because I have two small babies, I will not leave, nor will I put them in the care of someone else so I can work. I will stay in this relationship but I am not sure I can love a man who behaves this way.

At that moment I felt only animosity toward him. I was determined that my children would have the life I intended for them to have, and I realized with an overwhelming sadness, that *I* did not matter to him.

I intended for this to be a true marriage, but it was not. I saw now that my children, not he, would be my life, and I began to believe what I had been told, that God would punish me if I married out of the Church. This unhappiness may be my punishment, but I would not allow my children to be punished.

I wanted to lash back at him, confront him with the same venom he spewed at me, but could not. Instead, I absorbed his angry words and internalized what I should have expressed, all in the name of keeping peace. I had no idea of the terrible pattern I was setting or the cost I would pay. I needed and wanted to confront him, but was unable to.

Instead, I would live with the damaging effects that resentment, and the feeling of being enslaved would have on my health, both emotional and physical, while inside, I longed to be the person I once had been.

I wanted to be again, that happy and outgoing person that made friends easily and was comfortable in a crowd instead of this wife who had become the opposite. I always looked for the higher qualities and basic goodness in the people I associated with and my friends were like that. I was cheerful and loved people and a good party. I loved babies and children, things of beauty, nature, being in love and the movies. I simply loved life. I was almost always happy.

Something vital had gone from me.

CHAPTER 9

AS THE "REAL ME" slowly receded into the background I began to function on automatic pilot. I cared for the children, loved them and gave them as much attention as I could. I tried to be the proper wife, kept an orderly home, entertained when appropriate, and in general appeared to be the average doctor's wife. I fulfilled my duties and lived the life that was expected of me. And as long s I did not upset the apple cart, life was normal. The person I used to be gradually disappeared.

Charles family visited frequently, and soon his young adult nieces and nephews came for extended visits while job hunting or attending local Colleges. Our two babies had taken over the study and we decided to build a larger, more adaptable house in the newly developed section of Chesterbrook Woods in nearby McLean.

I drew the floor plan based on our present needs and with a thought for the future since we would live in this new house for the rest of our lives. We hired an architect to put my drawings into a workable plan, but it took us over a year to finalize them.

In the meantime, I became pregnant with our third child, Jeffrey. There was anger, but no rage over this unplanned pregnancy possibly because building the house was uppermost in his mind.

I still got a lot of grief for having gotten myself pregnant again, but there were no months of silence from Charles, as I would encounter in future pregnancies. Jeff was born one month after we moved into the new house on Laburnum St. He was the easiest one of all and the best baby. Not colicky, he slept thru the night early, was always happy and very cuddly. Those were very busy years for me, but I adored my little family, and their presence proved to be the perfect buffer.

With the new house and new baby, life seemed to be better temporarily and I felt that Charles had finally come to accept the reality of our life. There were some peaceful years for a while, but not what I would call happy. He expected quiet when he was home and that was almost impossible with three little ones. About this time, I noticed he played more golf and was gone for longer periods of time. It suited me fine, life flowed more easily when he was not around.

We probably had about five years of reasonable normalcy but only because I did not cross him. It was during these years that I began to search for meaning and a way to change things. Keeping peace was very stressful, and I needed answers as it was not normal to live like this.

But anything I did outside of my expected duties in the house was unacceptable to him. However, it did not stop me from searching, I just had to keep it from him and was not able to discuss my interests with him either.

I also noticed during this time that Charles was drinking more. And as it slowly increased, so did his anger and unreasonableness. Gradual behavior changes are not always recognized in a busy life.

CHAPTER 10

FEAR OF BEING humiliated can control your life, and while I never actually believed he would reveal my *horrible secret,* Charles, who had been insistent that we never discuss my past, continued to make reference to it in a manner that I felt threatening. One evening on the way home from the Country Club where we had attended a Medical Society Dinner/Dance, he made a comment that re-enforced my fear.

I had been complimented in front of him several times that evening. Once, on the silk evening dress I had made. Again, on my dancing, and then by the wife of a senior Physician for something I had done in the Medical Auxiliary. I thought this would make him proud, and maybe it did, but he wanted to send me another message.

On the way home, I told him I had enjoyed the evening, which I had. "Would they still think you were so wonderful if they knew what you really were?" he said.

I was floored. "What I *really* was?" I asked. "What do you mean?" "You know what I mean," He said, turning his head and looking at me out of the corner of his eye for a second while continuing to drive. It was the first of many such responses I would hear whenever anyone paid me a compliment.

Later, I would go out of my way to avoid a complement if he was nearby. My insides would tighten and I held my breath, dreading the response. On a subconscious level, I probably believed what he was saying, so felt I did not have a right to contradict him. On a conscious level, I thought he was being sadistic, and felt crushed that he would continue to remind me of my low self worth.

Overall, Charles behavior was inconsistent and confusing. I thought we had put the past behind us. He was the one who insisted that I never bring the subject up. I was integrating myself into his *proper world* and thought I was respected for who I was. Yet, he used the past to harm me. Just when I felt good about myself, he deflated and hurt me.

Was I going to be put down every time someone paid me a compliment? I could not imagine what was behind his words, but more important, what was going on inside him? Why would a respectable, competent physician feel threatened by *me.*

You would think he would be proud, not jealous, of his wife, I simply could not understand his behavior so chalked it up to the fact that he had a couple drinks. That evening, I had not done anything to displease him. I had made a beautiful dress, knew how to dance, which he did not, and went to the Auxiliary meetings because it was required of Physicians' wives.

I had not yet learned that anytime I began to exert myself, either through conversation, or performing a task, he saw it as a threat.

It never occurred to me that he could be insecure. He was a well-respected surgeon, an excellent golfer and had lots of friends. His ability to not only meet influential people, but connect with them, was remarkable, and he could get anyone to do anything for him. Him insecure? No way.

I soon found I could expect a similar response from him whenever I undertook a project where an element of appreciation might exist. An example occurred while I was doing volunteer work for Chuck Colson's Prison Fellowship.

I fell into it quite by accident, but found the work in the fledgling ministry very rewarding. One day Chuck called me at home regarding an issue that needed clarification, and Charles answered the phone.

When I got home, Charles said to me with a mocking tone in his voice, "Your new boyfriend called and wants you to call him as soon as you can. So now it's *Chuck*, is it? You're on a first name basis with Mr. Colson, isn't that nice." And than in a more commanding voice, "Tell him to stop calling you at home."

I had no idea what Charles might have said to Chuck Colson, but knew he was capable of anything. I was mortified at the prospect he might have come across as the jealous husband he was, and further humiliate me.

When I got back to him, Chuck apologized for calling me at home. I told him it was quite all right, but sometimes my husband can be rude. Chuck laughed and assured me he had more on his mind than a rude husband and told me to forget it.

One day Charles said to me, out of the blue, which made me realize that he *had* been thinking about it," Maybe Mr. Colson would like to know what you really are."

Any time I seemed to be UP, he would need to bring me

back down. I realized that I needed to be out of the house occasionally, doing something productive. Otherwise my self worth was going to be continually eroded. I was used to interacting with people and needed this outlet.

And he must have known this, which is why he resented my involvement outside the house. I never understood his need for control...I was entitled to an outlet as he was with his golf. At first he would question why I wanted to go somewhere, later on, I would be forbidden to go.

If he thought that I was compliant, he was sadly mistaken. Even though I followed his orders somewhat, I was probably more passive aggressive than obedient. I already found out that a normal discussion with him was impossible and my questions of "why" would be ignored, so I was going to do what I could on my own. I followed the path of least resistance, but life still became a game of wits, always maneuvering so I would not upset the apple cart while attempting to do what I needed to.

I found myself walking on eggs. Half afraid of doing something that would incur his wrath, or worse yet, embarrass someone else because of me, I weighed every thing I did, practically. As time went on, I did become more involved outside the house and as Charles' disapproval of anything I did 'outside the house' grew, I became more uptight because I never knew what would trigger a negative response from him, but worse, what he might say or do the person involved, and he did not seem to care how it made him look. But *I* did.

Despite the rebuffs, I continued to do whatever would enhance my sense of worth.

I became involved in the children's schools because Charles once told me to "get over there and find out what they are teaching our children and see what's *really* going on."

I went, I saw, I got elected. I was put in charge of implementing various functions, and ended up being on the Parent's Board of two schools. This was a constant source of discord with him, but it was too late. By now, I was in good standing with the faculty and the other parents, and had a protective wall of approval around me.

One evening I attended a Parent's Board Meeting that included the Headmaster and Officers of the Governing Board of the school. After the meeting ended, a faculty member who was a good friend and another parent invited me to join them for a beer before going home. I told them I'd better get on home but they succeeded in convincing me to go with them.

I stayed a bit longer than expected and found myself locked out of the house when I got home. I had a key but he had secured the dead bolt which we rarely used. I went around to the front door and eventually to every door to the house. Afraid of waking the children at this hour I did not ring the doorbell. Then I noticed movement in the house, it was Charles. He had apparently been following me from door to door, but I had not been able to see him. Just as I was about to ring the doorbell, —he could see me thru the glass— he opened the door.

That was my punishment for being out so late. Once later on, he did the same thing when I told him I was bringing two of my lady friends home for a drink after a yoga class. Embarrassing and humiliating.

Nothing much more was said until the following week when the Headmaster stopped me in the hall when I came in to work in the library.

"Your husband paid me quite a compliment the other day," he said.

"Really?" I said. "What was it?"

Laughing, he asked me where I went after the Board Meeting the other night. It seems Charles had called this newly hired Headmaster at home and asked him, "Is my wife there with you?"

I was mortified.

"Not to worry, let me tell you what I said to him." Dick had a wonderful sense of humor and told me how the scenario went.

"Honey," he said to his wife, lying next to him in bed, "check and see if Nancy Hannan is in here with us. Nope, she's not under the sheets, don't see her anywhere, do we honey? I'm sure she'll turn up...why don't you just go back to bed, Dr. Hannan."

That's how it was. I never knew what Charles would do or say, he was that unpredictable. Driven by his chronic anxiety and need to dominate, he always had to know where I was. It was distrustful and humiliating.

Still, I avoided the Ladies Bridge groups, did not get involved with the neighbors, did not sit around the Country Club pool, did not play tennis or golf, both of which I wanted to, and joined no women's groups other than those connected to my husband's profession.

His demeaning words still hurt, still cut deeply into my self-image, despite the positive re-enforcement from outside, and I could not do anything to please him. It was only when in the company of others that I felt OK about myself, and even then, the recurring voice in my head said," If they really knew what you were, they would not think you are so great."

I sometimes felt that I was betraying my friends and associates. I felt like a phony.

More and more I found that whenever my self-esteem seemed to be on a good level, it would be brought to the edge of a cliff, and in a single moment, with a word or gesture, be pushed over into the bottomless crevice below. That is what it felt like.

If he saw that I was enjoying what I was doing, things got worse. I soon stopped sharing things with him.

With my sexual energy looking for a place to go, I began to sew. I found joy in working with beautiful fabrics, and designing my own clothes. I was familiar with the finest fabric stores in town and came to know the owners well.

One day, at the request of the owner of a store I frequented in McLean, I visited her Watergate shop. As I came thru the door, BZ greeted me with, "Nancy, I am so glad to see you. I am very busy right now and there is a customer here who needs help and it may take a little while, do you have time to help her? I know you can do it, if you have the time. She needs advice selecting patterns and fabrics for her dressmaker. The woman has a high profile job so keep that in mind."

I did have the time and this is what I loved doing. The woman was delightful, with impeccable taste and I was honored that BZ asked me to help her. After we made the selections, including all the accessories she would need, the customer thanked me profusely and left.

BZ waited for the door to close and watched her customer walk down the street. She then turned to me and said, "I purposely did not introduce you because you were a customer and out of deference to her need for privacy, thought it best. That was Rosemary Woods, Richard Nixon's private secretary."

When I got home and told Charles about it, his only comment was, "What were you doing in DC?"

"BZ wanted me to see her Watergate shop, and then asked if I would like to manage it for her." I was honored that she considered me capable of doing this, but had no intention of accepting because I knew Charles would not approve and the children were too young.

I was astonished when he told me, "You should take the job." I did not take the job, although I would have loved to, but the children were too young and I did not have the time that the job required.

I did not know why he always had to know where I was, or why he called home numerous times of the day, or would go to the places I frequented looking for me. I thought he did not trust me, why else would he check up on me all the time...it was very hurtful so I made it a point to always tell him where I was going to be. How long before he would trust me...I trusted *him*.

I still had not learned to read the signals. He was no longer the attentive man I thought cared so much, but had become the man who needed to know my every move. He needed to know where I was, *because he did not want me to know where he was*.

If I was in a fabric store in DC for five days a week, he would know exactly where I was. The light was beginning to come on, but it would be awhile before it really lit up the room.

I later realized his insecurity did not come from his outer world, but from his own inner struggle. A struggle that only became obvious to me years later. Charles' ease with critical words was a sharp contrast to his apparent inability to discuss sensitive issues. I was never able to get him to talk about what was really bothering him. I would need to decipher the clues on my own because I needed to know what I was dealing with, so I *could* deal with it.

Hurtful words that can never be retracted stay with you, maybe brushed aside to ease the momentary effect, but always deepening the wound. I would have been better off being hit once a month instead of the daily, demeaning *words* that were just as destructive as a blow to the head.

In order to lessen the *blow,* I would go out of my way to avoid any compliments, sometimes being rude by walking away or changing the subject if he was nearby. I one time said to him that "I am always flattered when someone praises *you,* why can't you be glad when someone praises me?" No answer.

I was no longer 'Sadie LaDu', the endearing name he called me before his enchantment wore off. He was now referring to me as 'Sister Suzie." It was a name that exuded contempt, as when he would say to me: "As for you, Sister Suzi, the next time you..." and a threat or insult would follow.

I would say back to him, "My name is Nancy."

Sometimes I would look back on our early days and wonder: *How did we end up here?*

The truth is, the changes that began to erode the marriage were gradual. At first, the hurtful words came only after he had been drinking. Though, I have to say, even realizing what fueled them, they had the same effect as a legal document...in my mind, they were legitimate.

Before we were married, I never saw a personality change in him even after a drink or two, and we often had more than one drink. As his private world became more complex with children and a home and responsibilities, his drinking escalated. It was common practice for us to have a drink before dinner and then a glass of wine with dinner, but as he drank more, I drank less.

I abstained when I was pregnant, mainly because even the smell of alcohol bothered me. And when the children were small I was very careful to limit what I did drink.

One summer evening, I was peeling potatoes at the

kitchen sink. Charles walked over, and reaching around me, put a martini in my hand. "Thank you," I said and he walked back into the family room. I started to say something to him but he was already gone. I wanted to talk, to have him say something to me, to connect. "He'll be better next week after we get to the shore," I told myself, "it'll be like old times once we're away from here." It was always better when we went to the Jersey Shore.

As was our habit, we would sit down and have a drink at the end of the day. I enjoyed it when there was someone to talk to. *drinking just to drink* was not good, especially with small children around. And that evening I decided that once we got to Avalon I would no longer drink anything because I did not want the children to see me drinking every day.

Charles had begun to drink more than usual and his personality began to change with the second and always with the third one. He became mean, caustic, and just plain nasty. I thought if I stopped altogether, and he had no one to drink with, he might cut back. For over three years, I did not touch a drop of alcohol and did not miss it.

That was when he began to stop by the club before coming home, and I noticed he stopped buying alcohol for the house. *A dominant clue that I should not have ignored.*

Something else was going on and again, I tried to figure out what I was dealing with. The verbal abuse had escalated and I was becoming more and more distraught. The effect on the children concerned me and I began to seek help from a variety of sources.

I was led to books that I could resonate with and I found a compassionate, understanding friend in Fr. Tom Gavigan, the Jesuit pastor of Holy Trinity Church in Georgetown. Fr. Gavigan, who was my Spiritual advisor for many years, once suggested I read Dag Hammarskjold's book, "Markings."

Dag Hammarskjold was Secretary General of the United Nations from 1953 until he died in a plane crash in 1961. He was a remarkable statesman, universally known and respected. The book is a compilation of his diary and journal dealing with his own spiritual growth. It was an incredible help to me.

In another session with Fr. Gavigan, he said to me, "God intends for you to be happy."

Well, then, God, I thought, *the Church says I have to stay married, so show me what to do.*

In all those years, I was never able to tell him about my 'horrible secret'...

When he told me to consider leaving Charles, I told him I could not. I felt it was wrong to run away from the problem, I wanted to fix it. Besides, I had no access to any money, no place to go and if I went to an attorney, I would be overruled. It was the sixties and a woman with children could not just pick up and leave because she was unhappy.

But I needed to find purpose in my suffering. Because I did not talk about the abusive behavior, and rarely spoke of these happenings or my feelings, I thought no one had any idea that our life was any different from theirs. Charles drinking was now another secret I had to keep, and for a good reason.

We continued to attend medical meetings two or three times a year. They were almost always held at golf resorts which seemed to placate Charles and he was fine most of the time. As his moods deteriorated, however, and the alcohol increased, I dreaded going with him because of the public abuse and my inability to stop it.

On one occasion, while checking out at the Greenbriar Golf Resort in Hot Springs, WVa. Charles called me over to the counter, "What's this charge you put on the bill? Who gave you permission to buy anything?" He then carried on for a few more minutes before realizing that some of the physicians we knew were standing nearby, checking out also, and could hear him. The charge was for a thirty-dollar item I bought in the gift shop. His golf fees were in the hundreds.

Any other woman would have immediately pointed this out to him but I was so embarrassed I could not say anything. I was propelled back into the mode in which I lived because *you do not deserve even this this little trinket.*

It was becoming increasingly common for me to find myself wanting to be absorbed by the earth in public those days because he would embarrass me in front of others. The feeling inside was awful, but the awful thing was that I could not muster the courage to challenge him. I would usually just get up and go to the ladies room to avoid a public scene.

Another summer, we were again at the Greenbriar for a medical meeting. Either in the dining room or bar, not sure which, because the vile language being slung at me was continuous. I barely ate anything. When we got up to leave, Charles said he was going up to the Hospitality Room.

It was a warm summer evening and I was not in the mood to be around anyone, so I went out onto the veranda that fronts the old building, and sat on a rocking chair.

A moment later, I felt a hand on my shoulder and must have jumped because whoever it was, said, "It's OK," and called me by name.

As I looked up at the man standing beside me, I saw the concerned look on his face, and he said, "I took the liberty of asking the Maitre'd for your name. You should not have to put up with that kind of abuse."

I was taken back because I recognized the man. "Sam

Snead," he said, offering his hand. "Are you afraid of him? Has he ever hit you?"

"No, he's never hit me."

"Well, he will, one of these days, they always do. I just want you to know that if you have any trouble with him the rest of your visit here, you are to *immediately* pick up the closest telephone, no matter where you are, there are phones everywhere, and tell the operator, 'I need Sam.' They know how to find me and I will be there in two minutes."

I apologized to him for the disruption in the dining room and told him I was embarrassed but was afraid my husband would get worse if I had gotten up and walked out—which would have embarrassed Charles, and is what I wanted to do, but dreaded the outcome.

"All I can say is, take care of yourself and don't forget the phone." He then said, "Good Night," tipped his straw hat and walked away.

Up until now, I hoped that others could not hear what was being said, because Charles was not yelling, but they could see the anger on his face, and probably thought that I had done something wrong and deserved the tongue lashing. Now, I knew differently.

On the way home, I thought of Sam and his kindness, but dismissed his other words: "He hasn't yet, but he will, they always do."

I would find out later that Sam knew what he was talking about.

Eventually I stopped accompanying Charles to medical meetings, and began refusing his invitations to eat out. His abusive behavior in public became that bad.

I never told Charles about the Sam Snead incident. It was my private security blanket, along with Sam's encouraging words and the kindly touch saying, "someone cares."

It gave me the first bit of energy and motive to look for the answers I needed...and for a way to change my life.

CHAPTER 11

IT STARTS WITH A PUSH

TO BETTER UNDERSTAND my husband, I felt I needed to know what drove him. In view of the fact he would walk away rather than answer me, I still tried to find out what was behind his erratic behavior. I believed if I knew, we could fix it.

There were many times I wish I had done things differently, but I was too afraid of the consequences. If something displeased him he would always retaliate. While I never knew what form it would take, I always knew he would do *something*.

Up until now, the changes that eroded the marriage had been gradual, but in the seventies, they rapidly escalated. The most dramatic changes occurred when I was pregnant with our fourth child. Charles' fury over my being pregnant sent me into a depression that forced me to take action.

I realized I needed to see a professional in the mental health field...

Up until now, the abuse was only verbal. He would come through the door like a roaring lion, and out of context, would tell me that "it is your inadequate personality, you do not know how to run a house, you don't know how to raise children, you can't handle the help, you never pay your bills on time."

Those words were his mantra...I heard them over and over, and over.

However, it was the last one that sent a red flag up, because I had no access to the check book, *he* paid the bills, and not always on time...that belonged to him, not me, and later on I realized that all those other things he attached to me, really belonged to him.

I *did* know how to run a house because I was doing it and I knew far better than he, how to raise children because as the oldest of eight, I had some experience. Maybe I did not handle the help as he would, but since he grew up with multiple servants, he could show me.

What made me feel inadequate the most back then was his perpetual complaining about the cleanliness of the house. It was endless. Every day he would call my attention to something...every single day! So, rather than run the house in a more efficient manner, I would do the things he was more likely to complain about first.

Stupid? No, *insane.*

I should have told him that I do not interfere in his office, so do not interfere in the running of the house, but I did not because I was reluctant to hear his mocking reply.

While I considered myself a good housekeeper, these daily criticisms further eroded my self-esteem and some days, I just could not seem to function at all.

I reminded him that I had a German mother who thought that scrubbing down the walls was appropriate, and an elderly relative who called me her "crazy clean cousin."

Once I asked my sister if her cleaning lady had an extra day. She did, but only came to me the one time. She told my sister that it was too confusing working for me. All she did was 'clean over the clean' and she 'never knew when she was finished.'

Something else was behind this cleaning frenzy of his... it was not about my housekeeping skills, nor was it about his need for everything to be perfect...but I thought it was.

Gradually, my frustration turned to indifference and I began to run the house as I saw fit and a bit more efficiently, disregarding his orders. When he saw that his 'list of chores' was not high on my list anymore, he started a new tactic.

The *When are you gonna* mode clicked in. Again, I needed to develop my own strategy for dealing with this interference and subsequent criticism, which I began doing. The fact that I was now challenging him created a new wave of resentment and I believe it is what ultimately let to the escalation of abuse.

For years I had followed the path of least resistance and it had become a pattern. But, I have a built in rebellion gene of my own and it began to surface. If I was passive aggressive before, I became even worse. The more he ordered me to do something, the deeper I dug my heels in.

I had had enough. It was time to step up to the plate and swing the bat. This team had other players on it besides a pitcher, and I was more concerned about them than myself. The children were growing up and mattered more than I did.

Constantly trying to protect them from him and his wrath, I was still unable to shield my children from the irreparable damage caused by the world they lived in at home.

This became evident when I noticed that our two year old would often slide off his chair before he finished his dinner and go hide. I found him one day lying under the sofa in the adjacent family room with his arm around our cairn terrier who was lying beside him. I realized that Jon had a full view of the driveway from the table and could see when his father's car approached.

Both he and the dog were disturbed by the loud yelling. I only wished my husband would treat the children as well as he treated the dog. One day I overheard Charles call the Vet to tell him that Belmont was depressed...what could we give him! The *dog* is depressed? What about the rest of us?

This was the tuning point in my resolve to do something about behavior that was having such an impact on a two year old. The older three children were born within three years and there was a seven-year gap between them and Jon. The older ones had not experienced this behavior until now. Things had dramatically changed in the past two years.

In fact, it was around the time of my pregnancy with Jon that I saw the dramatic changes in my husband. Mostly, his violent mood swings and his coming home mid afternoon to nap, requiring absolute quiet. The phones had to be turned off, Cara could not play her guitar, the dog could not bark, I could not run the vacuum, the neighbor's collies could not run across our front yard.

It was unreasonable to say in the least. An insane way to live and I needed answers.

During these years the children saw little or no affection between Charles and me, and this bothered me because it was essential if they were to learn how to relate to a future spouse.

Looking back, I often wished that I had spent more time with the children and paid less attention to Charles demands.

Instead, I found myself doing all the 'things' that would keep him from yelling when he got home. Knowing he was jealous of the children, I wonder now if he was intentionally keeping me from spending my time with them.

My only resolve and hope came as I looked forward to our month at the Jersey Shore. He was more himself up there, or rather, more like he *used* to be. It was sad to see how deeply the marriage had sunk.

My walks by the ocean where I could talk to God were very important to me and I would get up early each morning to walk the beach and watch the sun come up by the beautiful sea. I wrote my poetry while up there with no fear of it being seen and mocked and always found a safe place to hide it before he came up on the week-ends.

Sometimes I would get a kiss when he arrived at Avalon, but soon could not remember the last time he kissed me hello at home. How can you kiss someone when you are yelling at her?

I did not realize how much I missed affection until one evening when a good friend who lived down the street invited us to his home to meet some out of town friends. The children were now old enough to leave alone for a short time...so Charles and I walked down the hill to his house.

A bit later, I said I was going up home to check on the children. "I'll be up shortly" Charles said, and I started to leave. The gentleman house guest said, "you shouldn't walk up alone, it's dark out and there are no street lights, I'll walk you home." So he and I left together. We walked up the hill and when we got to the house, I reached for the door, thanked him for walking me home, told him I really appreciated it and said "Good Night."

He put his hands on my shoulders, kissed me on the

forehead, and said Dave had spoken about us so much, it was a pleasure to finally meet, and he walked back down the hill to Dave's house.

I went inside feeling the warmest glow I had felt in a long, long time. I recognized how a simple touch can make you feel special. Charles 'only touch those days was a pinch that hurt. He would stand behind me while I was cooking, reach around and pinch me in a very sensitive place.

The fact that I told him it hurt and asked him not do that again seemed all he needed to continue doing it. He only stopped after I swung around one day and hit him quite hard. The look on his face was one of shock...he never expected me to do that, but it hurt and I was angry. That was the end of the pinching.

It was not long after the pinching stopped that he shoved me one day while I was standing in the kitchen. He wanted to walk past me, so gave me a push out of the way. "If I am in your way, ask me to move, don't just shove me!" I said.

He replied, "I'll shove you all I want to." And headed down the hall to his study.

Again, I wish I had told him, "never do that to me again" or had pushed him back, but I think I was afraid of what he might do, given his strange behavior.

During those years, I did think of divorce, but it was out of the question at the time. I kept my RN license currant but had no intention of leaving him, going back to work and trying to educate the children. I knew if I left him he would not pay for college. Years down the road, I was proven right.

In my family of origin, going to College was not as important as getting a good paying job, a mindset from the Great Depression. I was determined that our children would be educated and I was willing to stay until they were.

The price I paid for staying was heavy. I was determined to continue to search for meaning and purpose in my life, but anything I did along those lines was threatening to him. I did yoga for relaxation and learned to meditate. Both had a quieting effect on me and I felt much better, but the problem was finding the quiet time to do it at home.

He hated my yoga classes, and ridiculed anything else I did.

He absconded with my books and journals, took them to the Country Club and read my notes to his buddies in the locker room. I found this out from the other wives. Everything I wrote had to be hidden. Even the notes I might scribble on the margin of a book were fair game.

I felt betrayed. My privacy was invaded. It was no different than my mother on the phone telling her friends personal issues about me years ago.

The more independent I became, the more threatened he felt. And soon this threat reached a point where instead of talking to me about it, he would simply lash out. Often, I had absolutely no idea what was bothering him.

His intolerance for my independence finally reached a climax one day. As he was going out the door that morning, he turned around and said to me, "I'll be home about eleven this morning, I need to talk to you about something. Please be here."

It was rare for him to discuss anything, so I was actually looking forward to what it was he wanted to talk about...He seemed to be in a good mood when he left and was not angry or upset so maybe this was a sign that things were improving.

At eleven, he came thru the garage and into the family room, *and just stood there.* Without a 'hello' or any introduction, he blurted out, "Unless you revert back to the person

I married, I am going over to Holy Trinity Church and have Father Gavigan dissolve this marriage." I had to stifle a laugh.

"Father Gavigan cannot dissolve this marriage, Charles, because we were not married in the Church, to begin with. Secondly, I am not the person you married any more than you are the person I married. People change, we grow."

"Well, I will not tolerate your new found independence!" he said. "Where do you get the idea you can speak out like you do...have your own opinions about everything?"

"You are getting a little too bold. Talking to Judge — OL — like you did at the Club last week. What do you know about anything? You are my wife and you do not contradict me. You do not voice your opinion in public! Do you hear me?"

"I hear you and I will speak out when ever I need to. You cannot tell me what to think or say as long as it is socially acceptable." "Well, it is not acceptable to me," he yelled. "And in the future, you will keep your thoughts to yourself."

"Charles, on second thought, why *don't* you go over to Holy Trinity Church and talk to Father Gavigan? Tell him you want to dissolve this marriage. It will be as effective as your forbidding me to have an independent thought and expressing it."

"And if you *do* want to dissolve this marriage, go right ahead, it ceased to be a marriage long ago." He turned around and walked out the door.

I could not believe he was serious...It was almost comical if it were not so medieval. But the matter was not settled. I challenged him. He would have to respond.

Because he never mentioned it again, did not mean he forgot it.

His disparaging words were a daily menace and eroded any feeling I had left for him.

There were many examples of his obsessive jealousy, all unfounded, and were grounded in his own insecurity, nothing else.

One evening, we had gone to one of our favorite upscale restaurants in Georgetown. Near the Campus, it was a favorite spot for the Georgetown group and we always saw people we knew there. As we entered, the Chief of Surgery who had been a long time friend of Charles was sitting alone, having dinner. He asked us to join him.

"Sorry, but we have reservations in the back room." Charles said. When we got to our table I suggested we might have joined John because he looked lonely. "He eats here by himself every night, he's used to it." Charles added. After a non-communicative dinner, and as we were leaving, Charles and I again, passed John who was still sitting in his booth. This time, he said," Come on, it's early, have an after dinner drink on me."

Charles reluctantly sat down, we ordered cordials and then John said," How is it that every time I see you two, Nancy looks younger and you look older, Charlie?" John was notorious for his sometimes caustic sense of humor, few were ever offended by it, but it threw Charles into a rage.

He suddenly grabbed my arm, slid out of the booth and said, "We're leaving!" I pulled myself free and John told me to "sit back down." Charles said he was going to get the car and for me to be waiting outside. "You don't have to put up with that behavior. You just sit here and wait for him to come back in...I can't believe he got that upset over my comment... doesn't he have a sense of humor?" "Not if it is about him," I replied.

What followed next was the most bizarre behavior I ever saw in him. He came flying back into the restaurant, grabbed me by the arm and forcefully dragged me out of the restaurant, shoving me into a diner, and then shoved me into the swinging doors and out the main entrance. I have never been so humiliated in my life. What in the world were all those people thinking, and we knew many of them.

I was terrified, but had no choice but to get in the car. "If you are this upset", I said, "Please let me drive." "Shut up!" he yelled at me. He drove over Key Bridge at a high rate of speed, narrowly missing the turn onto Lee Highway. I did not say one word for fear of further agitating him, but once we got into the house, I said to him, "What in the world was all *that* about?"

"That John has had his eye on you from the very beginning...even before we were married!" "But he's *your* friend," I said. "I only remember him as a Resident years ago, and we hardly ever see those people anymore. I didn't even know he was divorced until you told me tonight at dinner. *You are crazy!*"

The next day, John called the house and told me I needed to talk to someone about Charles behavior. "I'm concerned for your safety if he is that jealous."

The abuse escalated and I never knew what would trigger an incident. Often, I had no idea. Sometimes, he would burst out with something that happened days before.

One evening after the children were asleep, he was watching Monday Night Football in his study. I knew he would be occupied for a couple hours so I went across the hall to the living room where I sat down at a small desk in the corner to write some letters.

Busy writing, I suddenly felt him standing behind me. Without saying a word, he grabbed me by the hair and swung me around onto the nearby sofa. I don't know what he was saying, but he was agitated and angry. "What's the matter?" I said. "*What* is the problem?" I could not make out what he was talking about as he wrapped his hands around my throat and began choking me. I could not breathe, and tried to push him away, but he was very strong and I was having a difficult time getting him off me.

I still had the pen in my hand as I continued to try and push him away. The harder I tried to push, the tighter his hands on my throat. In one desperate, final shove, I extended my arms and the pen, still in my hand, hit an artery in his arm.

Blood gushed out, covering the sofa, carpet and both of us. I rushed to get towels to stop the bleeding, then put a pressure dressing on the arm.

"You need more help than a pressure dressing" I said, "and you better get it."

He was very quiet the whole time and said nothing, not even, "I'm sorry." Then he asked me how to get the blood up, he did not want the children to see it. I told him to use peroxide. I checked in on the children, who thankfully were all asleep, and went upstairs into the guest room, and to bed, leaving him to clean up his own mess.

The next day when Charles came home from work, I noticed he had a different bandage on the wound. He had gone to the ER to see if he 'needed sutures'. I did not believe that was the reason he went to the ER, but I let it go.

The push was the beginning. Should I have pushed him back? *Maybe...*Once I tried to hit him after endless accusations and he grabbed both of my wrists and immobilized me. He had been tormenting me in an uninterrupted pattern that was almost diabolical, and I was enraged. At times I felt he was possessed. He would get a look on his face that seemed almost demonic. There was something very wrong going on with this man, and I did not know what it was or what to do about it.

Still, I told no one what was happening...who could I tell? A *lawyer*? I actually did speak to one at the suggestion of a friend. I wanted to see if I could get Charles to move out and let the children and me stay in the house with out going thru a divorce. I told him the continuous false accusations of infidelity were only a part of the abuse.

He looked at me, leaned forward across his desk and said in a low voice, "Honey, when in God's name would you have time to have an affair, with all those children and all those things you have to do? He's just trying to keep you in line... some men are like that. Try to ignore him, he probably had a bad day at the office." He never charged me, but I had a feeling as I walked out of his office that he was laughing his head off.

A *priest?* Before I met Father Gavigan, I spoke with a priest who had been a long standing acquaintance of my friend, Jeanne. I approached him back when we were trying to get an annulment, and Jeanne may have recently told him we had gotten married without one. When I met him this time, his only words to me were, "You people do what you want and then come running to us for help." Nope, I wasn't going to go running back there again.

My *Doctors?* All of them were colleagues of my husband. I did approach a physician friend of ours for help once. I wanted to know if there could be something wrong with Charles, was he sick? What could I do about this behavior? He told me to make two martinis just before Charles got home and when I saw him walk up the steps for me to drink both of them. "At three in the afternoon? He follows the school bus in." This man was as insane as my husband but I found that no one took me seriously when I tried to get help, so I stopped asking.

My *friends or family*? Not back then. No one was going to confront a physician, especially one who had operated on them as a favor. How could I ruin his good name? He had too good a reputation among his peers, and I doubted that anyone would believe me.

Only later, much later, did I finally get professional help, and the most difficult part was having to tell the psychiatrist that I was an abused spouse, because it carried with it, yet, another stigma.

CHAPTER 12

WE MADE IT

IN APRIL, 1977, I was about to have our fifth child. The other four were easy vaginal deliveries, but this baby was large and breech, I was now forty-six and had a history of hypertension, so had no choice but to have a Caesarian Section.

Alone in the labor room, waiting for the blood work to be completed, I wondered where my husband was...he was nowhere in sight. When Jorge, my wonderful OB came into the room, I asked him if he had seen Charles, he said he had, and told me, "He'll be up in a few minutes."

I saw my husband just as I was being wheeled into the Delivery Room, but then he turned and started to walk down the hall. "Charles, aren't you coming in with me?" I called to him. "No, you'll be OK." I wanted him to at least act like he cared, to hold my hand while they were getting me ready... I could understand a lay person being a little squeamish, but he was a surgeon.

Being a former OR nurse did not make it easier, either. In fact, I think it is more difficult for us because of what we *do* know. I really needed his reassurance that I was going to be all right and wanted him to be there at least until they got the baby out. But he was gone.

Given our history, why I wanted him there with me in the first place was a mystery that took me years to unravel.

There was no time to think about Charles now anyway because Jorge had just come into the room and gave me all the reassurance I needed. "You're doing great," he said, "the epidural is working, the baby sounds good, and we'll have her out soon."

Jorge, whom I knew from his days as a Resident at Georgetown was a wonderful OB and I had the utmost faith in him. "We'll be making the incision any second now, Nancy," he said to me a few minutes later and I knew it should only be about ten more minutes before this baby would be out of my belly and in my arms. "Thanks, Jorge, it's reassuring when you tell me what you are doing."

It had been more than ten minutes, and I could feel the tugging, but no pain, and realized they were having a difficult time getting this large baby out. He sensed my apprehension when I pleaded with him to "Please, make a larger incision, Jorge, I don't care, just get her out safely."

"Her vital signs are good, so just try to relax a little, we're doing fine," he said. Jorge was able to keep me focused and I did not need nor want to think about the awful, troubling months that had preceded this moment.

Her vital signs are good. What a contrast to the vital signs of this marriage. The signs I was trying to ignore were not good, they were terrible.

My life with Charles, during the years our first four children were born had been an emotional roller coaster...at best. As he adjusted to the first two, life began to be a little happier. The children were good, happy and easy, and I loved my busy life with these two beautiful babies.

I survived the building of the new house while pregnant with number three, and Jeff's induced birth the month after we moved into the house. He was such a good baby I was certain that Charles would soon accept him, and he eventually did.

I now had four children. Three under three and a 43 year old. *I got this far*, I thought, *I will continue to survive.*

If there was a problem — and there so often was — I would want to discuss it. Charles would walk away, however — only to come back later and bring up the subject when it was out of context, probably after he had time to digest the issue.

I had no idea that his unreasonable demands on me were linked to his deep insecurity to money. It did not matter if it was ten dollars or two hundred, the accusing outburst was the same. I learned that it was not the lack of money, but *my* spending it that caused his anxiety. Like everything else, I learned it was a matter of control.

We both agreed early on, to send the children to private schools for a variety of reasons. Whenever I needed to talk to him about tuition or books or uniforms that needed to be paid for, he would routinely start to scream at me. "Where do you think the money is coming from?" he would shout.

I could not allow the children to repeatedly over hear these conversations. It was having an adverse effect on them.

I made it clear to him one day that we had to sit down quietly, and not discuss this in front of the children anymore. We had to put the money issue to bed.

His stock answer was that, "If you stay out of the stores, we'd have the money."

One year I decided to test his theory. He was still paying the grocery bill every month to Country Club Market where we charged our groceries, so I did not have to worry about food.

I decided that I would not make one single purchase in the department stores for three months. I extended it to four months, without a single purchase, hoping for some relief, which never came. When the bills came in each month, (he *rarely paid an outstanding balance in full*) he still yelled about the balance. I kept quiet for those months and just let his unfounded yelling roll off my head. I was waiting. He never even noticed that there had not been one cent spent in a store for four months.

By the fourth month, as he began his usual tirade, I was ready, and when I called it to his attention, his comment was, "See, you don't need to be spending all that money after all. You *can* get by without going into the stores."

"No, Charles, that is not the point," I said, "The point is, that you will scream at me at the mere sight of a bill, whether I have charged anything or not, and we *cannot* get by without spending money, and now, we need to buy the children some clothes, they have outgrown the ones they have."

"Well, I'll buy the boys' clothes," He said. And off he went to Brooks Brothers. He came home with three expensive blazers for the boys who were six, twelve, and fourteen. "Did you buy pants and shirts to go with them?" I asked. "No, they have those."

At their age, they would have outgrown the blazers in a few months. He spent triple what I would have spent for good quality elsewhere. I took the items back to Brooks Brothers and went someplace else. I found complete outfits that were just fine. This is typical of the games I had to play to make a point....

What was I not seeing?

The problem was obviously not money, but I had no idea what it was. From then on, if the children or I needed something, I would write a check and tell him to cover it. I was far too busy running a house and raising children to bow to his angst.

And so, I sucked up the angry words. I kept telling myself that by ignoring them, I had solved the problem.

I had not. What I had not seen was that by ignoring Charles' anger, I had created a much larger problem. I had distanced myself from him so far that I no longer cared. I was unable to deal with his unreasonableness and his accusing words. And on top of that, his attitude toward the children, and his increased use of alcohol, got worse.

I always blamed the alcohol, thinking, *If only he'd stop drinking he might become the wonderful man I first met, again.*

When the tension of whatever was plaguing him got too great, we were treated to loud outbursts that often sent the children into hiding.

Because of his disruptive behavior and the effect it was having on the children, I would often take them for long rides on the week-end. If they had activities on Saturday, I would take them with me shortly after Mass and breakfast on Sundays. I would look in the real estate section of the paper and make a list of lovely properties far from where we lived in McLean.

They seemed to enjoy these trips and would have lots to say about whatever property we would be looking at. I remember one particular day after one of our outings.

Jon, who was now four years old, was sitting in the kitchen while I was preparing a meal. "I hope we can buy that house we saw yesterday, Mom," he said. "It really was nice, wasn't it?" I said. "But it's too far away for Dad. He needs to be closer to his office and the hospital."

"I don't mean for him to go with us. He can live here and the rest of us can move out there away from him," *from a four year old*! I learned that the other children were hoping for the same thing. For several years, they would ask me if we (minus their father) could move away somewhere.

Over the years, I learned to get by on my own emotionally, and attempted to cover up for this volatile man in public. I no longer felt connected to him. In his world, as a physician, he was a god. And it took me a long time to figure out how small a role I played in the world of adulation he reveled in.

I went out of my way to prevent anyone from seeing the nightmare I was living...especially my family of origin. I never spoke to them of anything that went beyond what they could see for themselves.

And I realized that you do not have to be happy to be cheerful.

If I 'd thought I could keep minimizing my own feelings, stay out of Charles' way, just not rock the boat, and things would be okay...I was living a fantasy.

With each prior pregnancy, his erratic, hateful behavior became worse. He would not speak to me for months at a time. Somehow, he failed to see the connection of his need and the pregnancy.

Birth control pills had just come onto the market in the late sixties, and one day, my husband brought a pack home to me. (My OB was Catholic and forbidden to practice at a Catholic hospital such as Georgetown if he prescribed birth control.) After taking just one week of pills, I got so violently ill that I refused to ever touch them again. There were other methods of course—not good ones, in those days—and I even got pregnant on contraceptive foam.

Soon our intimate life came to a halt. Aside from the pregnancies, the marriage was on rocky ground and I seemed unable to find a solution to our unhappiness. Divorce was often on my mind and I came to the conclusion that it was the only answer. Still, I had many unanswered questions that frustrated me immensely.

I was left to wonder what was going on inside him. Why had this sexually needy man not touched me for two years. Why did he come home in mid afternoon to nap and demand quiet...was he ill? Why would he never answer my questions. He had become a stranger.

And I had become the dumbest wife in town....

The baby was still not out.

Charles should be in here, I thought...*Why won't he come in?*

But why did I want him to be here? He would be useless... Then I rationalized his absence. He still was under the impression he was not the father, and had rejected this child from the beginning.

The summer before, the children and I were at Avalon, as was our custom, and Charles would come up for long weekends. One week, he arrived about noon, mid-week...unusual. I was surprised to see him, and asked," Why didn't you let me know you were coming?" "Just decided to take an extra day off and come up early," he said. "Where are the kids?"

I told him they were still on the beach with orders to stay around the lifeguards' chair and I'd call them when lunch was ready. We were only two houses from the beach, anyway.

"Come on upstairs, I want to talk to you." "Why can't we talk here?" "Because if the kids come in I don't want them to hear us." I am thinking to myself, *if they come in, we can stop talking*, but so accustomed to doing what I was told, I went up with him.

He wanted to have sex. "After two years, you now want to have sex?" I said. "Is that why you came up, unannounced in the middle of the week? What's going on with you, anyway? Are you having a problem we should talk about?"

"Just come here and get in bed," he said. It had been a long time, and I had been patient after a friend told me her husband did the same thing, once. It was because he was having a sexual problem and was too embarrassed to talk to her about it.

Blindly, and in denial, I believed that to be the reason for the abstinence.

I argued with him that I was having my period and did not want to, not right now...later..."It doesn't matter," he said. *My husband had a 'right' and I was his wife, and if I withheld favors, he might go elsewhere.*

What I did not know, was that he had been *elsewhere* for a long time.

When the pregnancy was confirmed the following month, he was even more irrational than with the others. He knew better than to mention abortion to me, but something else was driving him, and I could not imagine what it was.

I found out several months later during an interview with the geneticist who Jorge insisted I consult—because of my age and the risk of a Downs baby—The specialist told us he could pin point the exact day of conception: And he came up with a date two weeks later than the only date I knew was possible. The date of Charles' surprise visit.

Not wanting to bring up matters that this doctor did not need to know. I simply said that "I know the exact date of conception and you are wrong."

"I am *never* wrong," he said.

Charles smiled. A strange, self-satisfied smile. "I knew I could not be the father. You were having your period at the time we were together."

That sealed the issue with him and he refused to believe me, even though he heard me say in front of the doctor, but for *his* benefit, "I have *never* been with another man since I have been married to my husband." *Never.*

That same geneticist, I found out later was self-taught, had no formal training in the field. He later went to prison for medical fraud.

It wasn't until she was two or three, that Charles admitted to recognizing family traits in this child. One day he was standing in the kitchen, staring at her while she was sitting at the counter eating her lunch. "I guess she really is a Hannan," he said.

It was far too late. Too late for him. Too late for her by

then. As a toddler, she had an aversion to him, and would run to me whenever he came near her. And it was too late for me.

I am convinced that a growing fetus is very much aware of what is going on outside of the womb. They are aware of rejection early on. There are many studies about this phenomenon and I found it even more revealing, when years later, I worked with adults who had been adopted.

As the tugging on my belly continued, I heard Jorge, in an unusually strong voice for him, speak curtly to the anesthesiologist. "Why do you have her in *trendelenberg!* I don't have the baby out yet!" He was referring to a position where the patient's head is lowered quickly to bring blood back to the brain. "Because her blood pressure is 80/50", he replied.

I heard Jorge reprimand him because I was awake and able to hear what he said.

I was feeling light headed, and was now, apparently, in shock. That took precedence over the surgery, and so, the anesthesiologist had dropped the head of the table.

The next thing I knew, I was having trouble breathing and fought the nurse when she attempted to restrain my wrists, which up to now, had been free. She was trying to prevent me from pushing away the oxygen mask that I did not want. And then I got very angry because someone had turned the lights up so bright they were blinding me. On top of that, this whole room full of people seemed unable, or did not seem to notice or care that I was sliding off the table. They were too busy doing something else — as I continued to slide until I did not feel myself on the table any longer.

Suddenly, I could breathe without any difficulty, I swung

my arms freely above my head and felt light as a cloud. I could see someone on an operating room table and doctors working on her, but I just roamed above it all and felt this light, exhilarating sense of peace. I liked it here. I could hear the frantic words, was aware of the people in the room, but only vaguely aware of what was going on, as I floated around.

I was out of my body, in a beautiful, free state, floating...

The next sound I heard was the cry of my baby and I suddenly felt a *thud* as I re-entered my own body. Then, I heard Jorge say, as he held up the baby, "Here she is, Nancy, and she's fine!"

One of the nurses released my wrists, and another put the baby on my chest. She was so beautiful. I looked at her and said, "We made it, Jenny, we made it." She looked right into my eyes and I saw this three minute old baby smile back at me.

"I have to take her now," the nurse said. "I only wanted you to see that she was perfectly healthy, you can hold her a little later," and then she and the other nurse left with my beautiful nine pound baby girl and headed for the nursery.

As they got to the door, I heard the nurse say, "Did you see this baby smile at her mother?"

"Newborns do not smile!" the other nurse said. "This one did, I saw it myself!"

Once home, life took on a different aspect. Friends came and went, brought food and gifts, and some stayed a bit longer than I needed. I resumed driving the car pool in ten days and we had Jenny baptized at Holy Trinity Church in Georgetown where the other four were baptized.

Belmont, our cairn terrier became a diligent watchdog. The children adored the new baby, and she and I continued to share the master bedroom on the main level for several weeks when we traded places with Charles who happily moved back down stairs to the master bedroom.

Her father paid little or no attention to the baby during this time and if she were to cry at night I would hold and rock her back to sleep so he could get *his* sleep.

From the moment I saw her in the delivery room, I knew what I needed to do, and these thoughts were now, uppermost in my mind.

To accomplish this task, I first wanted to talk to the children about it.

One day, while Charles was at work, I called the four of them, including Jon who was now seven, into the living room. "Kids, " I said," There is something I want to tell you. Dad won't like it, but you have a right to know."

And then I told them about their sister who had been adopted at birth.

"When I look at you," I said to Cara, who was now sixteen "and think that I have a daughter out there somewhere, who could be like you, I simply have to know her. And when I look at Jenny, I remember how I was not even allowed to see my baby back then, I must find her."

"I need to find your sister. She has a right to know her origins and I have a moral obligation to tell her, but first, I want to know how all of you feel about it."

"Mom, you have to find her!" they said. "Do you know where she is?"

They were all talking at once, but what I heard were the voices of approval.

"Oh, Mom, all these years, you must have been very sad."

one of them said. They could not imagine how sad I had been. "How will you find her?" they asked me..

I told the children that in three months she would be twenty-one and the documents I signed years ago, forbidding me to contact her, will no longer be valid. I will write a letter to the physician who delivered her and who arranged for the adoption asking him to see that she gets the letter for her that I will send him.

In it I will give her my name and phone number and address so she can contact me if she wants to.

And so, though my relationship with Charles was in the worst place possible, I now had a mission to find my daughter, and the timing was perfect. I put the marriage on hold, and with my children behind me, turned my energy toward a more important task. It took precedence over healing the broken marriage. The divorce could wait.

No longer would my conditioned mind be running my life. I was going to live in the present. I no longer had a secret hung over my head, a dreaded secret that had been used to control me. I was no longer a hostage to the past. I was not *what anyone else had done to me*, anymore than I *was something I had done*. I was Nancy Hannan.

These past few years, as I searched for meaning and purpose, I found a deeper, more spiritual life than the one imposed on me by the Church I was raised in. I embraced and came to know a more loving, compassionate, forgiving God. A God Whose presence I often felt.

In my newly discovered world I found that I must first forgive myself in order to be whole...

Eckhart Tolle tells us, "You cannot truly forgive yourself or others as long as you derive your sense of self from the past. You must access your own power which is the power of NOW, for true forgiveness. You surrender to what *is* and become fully present."

On that day I remember feeling an unbelievable, overwhelming sense of peace and joy. I felt not only the love of my children, but a very special bond to them. More than that, I felt *free*.

Later, when I told my husband about the meeting with the children and my intention to look for my adopted child, I mentioned it with the casualness of asking if he wanted dessert.

I really did not care what his response would be. For, with or without his approval, I was going to do what I had to do.

What I expected to be a simple solution to locating my daughter became far more complicated. And the next few years would become an ongoing tropical storm, making these past seventeen years feel like a gentle rain.

CHAPTER 13

AVALON, NEW JERSEY, 1977

IN JULY, we packed up the two cars as we did every summer and headed for the Jersey shore. It had been seven years since we'd had a baby with us, and it took some re-adjusting on my part to accommodate the extras. Jenny travelled well, and since I drove the station wagon, the baby in her bumper-protected porta-crib—which took up most of the backseat—came with *me*. Cara, who would keep an eye on her, sat back there with her, and Jeff sat up front. Mat and Jon rode with their father in his car along with Belmont, the dog.

Jeff was a sensitive kid and always had a calming effect on the family. I was glad he was with me. The lulls between Charles' worst mood swings were getting shorter, and things were becoming more unpleasant at home. More than once, Charles threatened to cancel our plans for the shore, but since he had already made a deposit on the beach house the previous summer he decided we could go.

He was still unresponsive to the baby who was now three months old.

Inside myself I'd determined that this was to be my happy summer of fulfillment. But it was not to be. Before we left home, I wrote a letter to the obstetrician who delivered my first child—the baby girl I'd relinquished to adoption—twenty-one years before. Along with the note to him I enclosed a letter to my child who was now an adult. I asked that he forward it to the proper address, since he knew who the family was.

He'd answered my letter almost immediately, stating that all his records had been destroyed years before, after he retired, and he had no recollection of the case. And even if the records had not been destroyed, he said, many of the babies he delivered were adopted and, as a matter of privacy, he'd never kept such records.

I found this hard to believe, so I called him. I reminded him that I once introduced him to my husband who had gone to Medical School at Jefferson in Philadelphia, and that the two of them discussed my earlier pregnancy, and that I had come to him again for my post-partum check after our first child was born. "You don't remember that?"

"No, I am afraid I do not."

I was devastated by his response. For years, I'd believed that a simple solution was available when she came of age. This physician was my only connection to her and I'd counted on his doing what seemed like a moral thing to do.

Given the climate of the times regarding adoption, he did

what *he* thought was the moral thing to do and that was to protect the adoptive mother.

I had no idea what to do next.

And so, as we headed to the beach, I had much to think about this month: What my next move was, and how to keep Charles calm. I was determined to enjoy my children and especially the new baby and to find time to walk the beach so I could talk to God. He would get an earful that summer.

We settled into the beach house and the kids were happy. They could relax, the rules were minimal, and they seemed to find the same refreshment that I did in the ocean. I realized I would not have the freedom I had been used to because of the baby, but at sixteen and fifteen, Cara and Mat were quite responsible.

One of the advantages of having a baby at the shore was that I now had a perfect place to hide my poetry and my journal...under the mattress of the baby carriage. Charles would never think to look there.

And so I wrote whenever I could find the time. And I read everything I could about adoption. I continued my early morning walks along the beach, but whereas in the past they were refreshing and restorative, this year they made me feel more desperate. All my years of 'knowing' that when she was twenty-one I could contact her through a letter I would send the doctor — ashes...blown away in a single phone call.

I prayed for direction, and I prayed for wisdom to know what to do about the marriage.

One beautiful morning, walking in the surf, its cool water lapping onto my legs, I stopped to look out onto the expanse of blue green sea. The sun was slowly coming up over the horizon and something shifted inside me.

Suddenly, out of my loneliness and isolation, I felt a

oneness with everything. There was peace here by the sea, and the sense of a great Presence. I felt that here, God could more easily hear me, even if I whispered.

But I did not whisper, nor did I calmly, or tearfully plead with Him that morning. I felt an energy that came from desperation. To my amazement I found myself commanding God: *LEAD ME TO HER, OR HER BACK TO ME.*

I have no place to start—no name, no agency, no person...NO ONE BUT YOU.

And then I asked for forgiveness for being so bold.

But later I would know: It was the intensity of my desire, the directness of my request, the specific wish that I wanted fulfilled and the emotion with which I spoke those words to God that would start the ball rolling.

I knew that I would have to do my part as well, and made a promise to God that I would do whatever I could to help. But there was nothing that I could think of.

I decided I would enjoy the month at the shore and, since I had no idea where to go from here, not think any more about the issue of my daughter.

I spent the month with our summer friends and my children during the week. When Charles came up for the weekend, we would take Jenny for long rides in her carriage in the evening.

Jon, who was now seven, always came along with us on these walks, and I had a feeling it was to make sure 'nothing bad happened.'

There was little conversation between my husband and me and never anything of substance. I felt he was tolerating this child he still thought was not his, and I never tried to convince him otherwise. It was his loss and my hurt.

He never brought up the search for my daughter, probably

realizing I was too busy with the new baby and had forgotten about it. The longer I could keep my intentions from him, the better, but I only *thought* he had forgotten it. He was waiting until I made the first move. But we were at the shore and everyone was having a good time so he would wait until we got home.

I would find out later, that shortly after he received my letter, the obstetrician called the adoptive mother and told her that I was looking for 'the child' and suggested she destroy any identifying papers.

CHAPTER 14

MCLEAN, VIRGINIA, 1977

WHILE I WAS disappointed and frustrated, I remembered my strong plea to God that day by the sea. I felt that somehow a deep connection had been made and that at some point, a door might open. But for the present I had nowhere to go for help and no idea how to search for someone without any identifying information. I despaired of ever locating my daughter.

Once back home, however, the peace I'd enjoyed at the shore wore off rapidly as Charles resumed his old ways. And then some.

From then, and for the next three years, my situation was horrible. Whatever had transpired before, got worse. The anger, the drinking, the yelling—it all got worse. The abuse that had been verbal, and minimally physical, now became physically obvious. I realized I needed to do something about it — but what? Now I had a new baby and leaving was even more out of the question.

As she grew, Jenny was a darling and the kids loved her, as did everyone else. On her first birthday, her father was a bit more attentive and my hopes grew. It was shortly after that when he made the comment, "She really does look like a Hannan." But otherwise he had little to do with her…or the other children. What a pity for him and her and all of us. As for me, the hurt went too deep for me to ever erase it.

He went all over the scale with his erratic behavior. Sometimes, more loving to the children and sometimes, more hateful. He was indeed a troubled soul.

During one of his outbursts, Jenny started to cry and I went to her crib and picked her up. I told him to go away and stop yelling, he was frightening her.

Charles was enraged over something. He came after me and, even though I was holding the crying baby in my arms, he swung at me, barely missing her, and hit me in the face.

Jenney was terrified, and clinging to me. I was frantic and could not imagine him expressing his anger with the baby so close. None of this seemed to bother Charles at all. Jon, who was standing nearby, looked visibly upset.

Later, alone in my room, I knew I had to do something about this. Jon's devastated, shaken look, and Jenny's terror were terrible.

I could not allow the children to witness any more brutality. But I did not know what to do. I could not get thru to him about his behavior and if I spoke to him about it, he would dump the blame back onto me.

The next year, Charles refused to go Cara's High School Graduation because he was mad about something. He was always mad about something, so nothing new there. He finally showed up, but sat by himself. We only saw him after graduation.

The following year, Mat graduated and as best as I can remember, he attended. But we never new *when* or *if*...whether it be a graduation, dinner, an invitation or Church. Life was about as unsettling as it could get.

I once went to a black-tie dinner dance alone because he refused to go at the last minute. I was co-chairman of the event, and needed to be there. I think this incident must have occurred before Jenny was born, because he and I did not go to many social functions after she was born.

As I look back at his behavior during these years, I realize Charles was rebelling against the life he did not want. What he *wanted* was to live a life separate from the family and I was aware of it long before I confronted him.

But by then I had learned that it was of no avail to confront him or to question him about anything. The only positive effect was that he now knew that *I* knew.

When I suspected he was using something other than alcohol, I tied the abusive events to his drug use. This was later confirmed.

It was during these years that an old family friend came back into my life. I was working with Chuck Colson's Prison Fellowship at the time, and some of the sessions were held over near Catholic University. When my mother heard I was going there, she insisted that I go by and see Father Murphy who had recently come back to the States after fifteen years in Rome, where he'd taught moral theology and was a peritus, or authority, on the Vatican.

"Father Murphy is now Rector of Holy Redeemer College," she said, "and every time I talk to him he asks about you. You must go see him."

Father Murphy had been a part of our family for many years. I was eight or ten when he first came to our home as a young priest. He and his mother soon became close friends of my parents and we saw a lot of Father Murphy those years, so I knew him well.

Still, I was reluctant to go visit him. He and I had had a falling out over the annulment years ago. Before Charles and I married, we decided to contact Father Murphy who was then living in New York, to see if he could assist us in getting Charles' first marriage annulled. He was well connected in Church matters, and I hoped he could help.

He met with us individually, and when I went in to see him, after he had already spent some time with Charles, all he said to me was, "Don't marry him...he's not right for you, forget him, there are more fish in the sea."

Angry at his seeming arrogance and indifference, I had little to do with him after that. I was very hurt.

But now, my mother had already told him that I would be by one day to say hello, so I reluctantly went.

Fr. Murphy was expecting me the day I stopped by and he opened the massive door of Holy Redeemer College himself. It was actually good to see him again and we had a very pleasant visit. My old animosity toward him forgotten.

I saw him frequently over the next two years and was able to talk to him about anything and everything. With him, I felt unconditional acceptance. I filled him in with the details of my life and he agreed with me about Father R. who was a confrere of his.

However, I never told him about the abuse, just that Charles had a drinking problem and we had a terrible marriage. Because he was so close to my family I was afraid he may say something and I did not want any of them to know.

I did not want my family to think ill of Charles because he had been good to them. He loaned them money, operated on family members, took in, my sister, Eileen when she ran away from home and subsequently sent her to college her first year.

I felt that if they knew my circumstances, they would blame me for his behavior. I protected Charles and my family and it never occurred to me to protect myself.

But now, I had someone I could confide in and he became my staunchest supporter until the day he died years later.

I no longer felt alone, and that comforting feeling enabled me to function on a higher level. "Murph", as we in the family so irreverently called him, was a prolific writer and he and I often had deep discussions on the subject. I once told him I wanted to write, but he said," You are a poet. Stick to that. Writing is a lonely life."

Once he became aware of the unpleasantness at home, 'Murph' said I needed to get away from the house for periods of quiet reflection and to replenish my energy. He suggested that the most obvious place free of the demands of my life would be sailing on the Chesapeake Bay, where he had the use of a sailboat that belonged to a retired Admiral friend of his near Annapolis. "You can take the baby"—meaning Jenny, who was now almost two—"over to your mother's for the day," he said.

So, I would take Jenny to Mom's, pack two lunches, pick up 'Murph' at Catholic University and head for Annapolis. Out on the bay, without a phone or doorbell or children, or an irritable husband, we could talk without fear of interruption. We talked about theology, the Church, God, my predicament, how I might find my daughter, and writing.

He was a pretty good sailor and an excellent teacher. Soon I was raising the sails, taking them down, and tacking across the bay. After two years of these outings, I had regained a lot of my old self-confidence and, one day, asked him if I could bring the boat in by myself. He looked at me with a questioning expression on his face.

"I know I can do it, *please, Murph.*"

"This isn't my boat, and what if...," He faltered. "OK, go ahead," he conceded.

And I did...without incident.

His presence in my life was uplifting—but more important I had some intellectual stimulation...something that had been missing for a long time. Ladies Bible Classes just did not cut the mustard.

"You want to write?" he said one day. "Then you need to learn how to edit. Here, take this home with you and red pencil any place I may be repeating myself." He then handed me a huge brief case. It was his new manuscript. When I handed it back to him two weeks later it had quite a few red lines in it. He laughed and said he knew it, but needed the word count. I felt a bit angry at the apparent waste of my time, but he had been able to keep my mind busy with something that would be advantageous to me later, while distracting me from that part of my life I could not change at the moment. He was a very wise man.

Charles disliked Father Murphy intensely. He was jealous of the time I spent with him, and I think he recognized that he himself could no longer agitate me. Because I had regained some of my own self-esteem I had learned to block him out.

This was an important lesson that I wish I had realized over the years. Up until now, I spent most of my time trying to fix something that was broken, trying to maintain a 'normal' home life, trying to be who I was not. Now, things were beginning to turn around. I was starting to feel good about myself.

While I did have other distractions over the years such as the schools, the Medical Auxiliary, and the Women's Board of the American Heart Association, they did not fulfill my need for acceptance on a personal basis.

Everyone needs to feel accepted unconditionally by someone close to them.

During those years under the protective arm of Murph I found myself receptive to whatever was in my path. While waiting in line in the Safeway one day, I saw a booklet on adoption on the turntable. I quickly put it under the bread I'd just set on the conveyor belt so no one would see me buy it. A few weeks later I saw an article in the Sunday supplement about the Adoption Forum of Philadelphia. I cut the article out and as soon as I could, I contacted them. They would eventually, point me in the right direction.

In the meantime, Charles had taken Jon out of the private boy's school the others had attended and enrolled him in a parochial school several parishes away. I would drive him to and from school. Jeff was now in the local high school and Cara and Mat were in college. One day I noticed that Jenny had picked up Jon's habit of hiding when Charles' car appeared in the driveway.

I would often find her behind the draperies, hugging Belmont who was now protecting *her*, or under the dining room table, which was her favorite place.

It was October, 1980, a beautiful day, as I drove over to pick up Jon after school. I had plenty of time before school was out so went into the Church. My heart was too heavy to carry by myself any longer. I was at the end of my rope, and needed to talk to God in a serious way.

I knelt down, close to the altar, trying to think of a reverent way to say the words in my head. There was little reverence, but tremendous faith, as I said to Him, "I will do *anything* You ask of me if You will get me out of this unhappy marriage."

I could never have imagined what God was going to ask of me, but in the next few years, as I faced one crisis after the other, it never occurred to me that I was doing what I promised I would do, *anything.*

Only later, would I look back and find that God did not waste any time answering my prayer. Within two days an event occurred that put the process in motion.

A male acquaintance from Philadelphia, who I had not seen for more than twenty years and who I had known through the medical community, called the house on a very busy late Halloween afternoon. I had kids to pick up from school, dinner to cook, costumes to put together for Jenny and Jon and the last thing I needed was company.

However, he was insistent that he see me before returning from his business trip, so I gave him directions to the house. He could be in and out before Charles got home and thus avoid an unpleasant encounter. But when he arrived, he said he wanted to meet my husband.

I called Charles at the Club and asked if he could come home early, then told him why.

By nine o'clock, Charles had still not come home so I called the Club again and asked that he *please,* come home as soon as possible. I realized that by now he probably would have had too much to drink and I did not want this old friend to see him in that condition, but the man was not leaving until he met my husband.

The children were long home from their trick or treating and I had already put Jenny to bed. Jon was sitting on the floor counting his treasures while Walter and I sat nearby having a cup of coffee.

Suddenly I noticed Charles standing in the doorway. I got up and attempted to introduce the two men when Charles, slurring his words, asked Walter what he was doing *"in my house with my wife?"* He may have been an abrupt German but Walter was always polite. "I came here to meet you and see Nancy's children," he said. "Well, you've met us, you can go now."

Charles then stormed out of the living room and headed down the hall toward the family room.

Walter looked at me with astonishment! "That is who you married!" I did not need to answer...he saw it in my eyes. I walked out of the room and followed Charles into the family room, hoping to quiet him down and ask him to please apologize for being rude.

I realized Charles was too *out of it* to be reasonable, but I intended to ask him anyway. While I was used to this behavior, outsiders were not. I was mortified that someone I used to know, someone who always thought highly of me, was witnessing this.

I remember starting to say something and the next instant, I was struggling to pick myself up from the floor but could not see because blood was running into my eyes. I was terrified that I was blind.

My ribs hurt and my head was pounding. He had knocked me out with a punch to the face and I had fallen over a large wooden magazine rack, fracturing several ribs.

Walter had followed me into the family room and witnessed what he did not have time to prevent, but I could hear him shouting at my husband. "If this was not your house I would kill you! You coward! A man never hits a woman."

While I was cleaning my face and trying to see where the blood was coming from, Charles quietly disappeared down the hallway, toward the master bedroom, and had gone to bed.

I called a very good friend of ours who was an attorney and told him what happened. He told me to leave the house and stay with a friend, or my mother that night and not come back into the house until Charles left. It was time to intervene and do something about his drinking.

He also told me to file charges. "If you don't, Nancy, he will kill you some day. At least the court will order him into treatment."

Jeff, who was sixteen, had not yet come home from the football game, but I was afraid to stay in the house any longer. I left him a scribbled, bloody note, saw that Jon got to bed, kissed him goodnight and told him to tell Jeff that I would call in the morning and let them know where I was. Jenny was asleep and missed all the excitement, thank God.

I realized I could not see to drive, so Walter said he would drive me if I could tell him where to go.

But he did not take me directly to my friends' house. He insisted on first taking me to an ER, where I did not want to go because Charles was well known at the local hospitals, and this would be embarrassing. "If you don't tell me how to get there, I will call 911" he said. So I told him. I was not about to argue with a former German SS officer.

The next morning I called Jeff and gave him my friend's address and told him how to get there. I asked him to please bring Jenny and Jon and as much clothing as he could pack for the three of them. "We are going up to Philadelphia and stay with Uncle Tommy until I know what we are doing." I told him.

I called my mother and told her what happened. "Not to worry, Mom, hopefully things will straighten out soon, I'll call you from Tommy's," I said. I only told her we had an argument and I was going to my brother's for a few days. I then called Cara and Mat at college and told them I would keep them posted.

The next day, the three children and I left for Philadelphia in my car and with Walter following in his. I knew my brother's place would be too small for the four of us, and we had discussed this before leaving for Philadelphia. Walter not only offered, but insisted that we stay in the house that he was renovating as an investment property. "I will only need the place for about two weeks," I told him. It was not quite finished, but it did not matter since we would not be there long.

Two weeks would give Charles time to get out of the house so we could come home, and the boys schooling would not be interrupted too badly.

As we drove away from the area, I thought of Dag Hammarskjold's words, "There is a point at which all things become simple and there is no longer any question of choice, because all you have at stake will be lost if you look back. Life's point of no return.

I realized at that moment, driving away from the home I designed, built and loved, that I *was not* "The house on Laburnum St." Nor *was I* "All the lovely things in that house." I *was not* "The president of the Medical Auxilliary", nor *was I* "Co-Chairman of the Heart Ball." *Nor was I* "Mrs. Doctor Hannan." I *was not* all those titles and objects from which I had drawn my identity.

I was Nancy Hannan, and I had just taken the first tortuous step in reclaiming that long lost identity.

CHAPTER 15

CONCLUSION

THE "TWO WEEKS" in Philadelphia became three years, years that I can only describe as a nightmare. While I found nice, clean places to live, I missed my lovely home in Virginia. I was also forced to move three times. My phone was tapped and I was followed most of those years. My mail was removed from the mailbox so my utility bills would be late and the utilities cut off. I found out later that Charles paid someone to continually harass me, hoping that I would go back home to Virginia.

He also threatened to kidnap Jenny and Jon, who were now three and nine. I took his threats seriously because the woman whom he hired to carry out his evil doings left a message on my phone to that effect. He had not paid her and she got even by telling me what he was doing.

As a result and out of fear he would do what he threatened, I never allowed Jon or Jenny out of my sight for those three years. I also stood my ground and refused to return to Virginia.

During that time, I was able to locate and meet my daughter.

Then, after three years away from McLean, and under pressure from my husband and the psychiatrist who had been counseling him (as a condition to my return), I did what most abused women do, I went back. The psychiatrist told me he had *identified* the 'problem' and, *corrected* it.

He convinced me that his years of counseling my husband were beneficial and I should try to salvage this twenty-year marriage. I had "too many years invested to throw away."

I knew the marriage was dead, but I wanted the two younger children to have a two parent family while they were in school. *How stupid can you be.*

The home I returned to was an indescribable mess. The property, unrecognizable. What once had been my lovely, clean, orderly home was a nightmare. The scene defied description. It put me into a deep depression as I tried to undo the damage to both house and property and myself. But it did confirm my long ago suspicion that Charles' obsession with cleanliness had nothing to do with cleanliness. He did not seem to know the difference between clean and dirt, order and chaos.

Those years of badgering me were nothing more than a matter of control, or an out of control case of obsessive compulsiveness.

Charles had gotten his 'housekeeper' back...and worst of all, I had lost my grounds for divorce.

I soon found myself in a pit of depression.

With the help of a different psychiatrist who had been a friend and known both of us for years, I was able to come up for air and finally breathe on my own. He and I delved into the life experiences that so greatly influenced my vision of myself, as well as my inability to change my life. He told me that as long as I saw myself as a *victim,* I was not going anywhere.

I had been seeing him for about two years, when, on one of my early Saturday morning visits to him, he told me that unless I left this toxic marriage, he could no longer help me.

"Well then," I responded, "ask your brother who is a judge to do something about the laws that prevent an abused woman from leaving without endangering her own legal rights."

The tension in the house had become intolerable. When the older children came home for holidays, *if they came home*, they did not stay too long. Cara was now living in Pennsylvania, Matt enrolled in Nankei University in China for one year before returning to William and Mary, and Jeff, at nineteen, drove to San Francisco where he enrolled in college. Charles told Jeff he would only pay for college if he came back to Virginia...so he quit school and went to work in order to support himself.

In January, of 1987 I told Charles that when school was out, one of us was moving out of the house. I refused to live like this any more. Since it was "his" house, he told me I would have to be the one to leave.

Using part of an inheritance from my elderly cousin, who had recently died, I was able to pay an attorney to draw up separation papers. After four miserable years back in Mclean, I finally left. Jenny, Jon and I moved into a townhouse in Falls Church for one year and then relocated to another one in Arlington where we lived for five and one half years.

During that time, I filed for divorce, which Charles contested, dragging it out for more than three years. The divorce was final in June, 1990, thirty years to the week we were married.

When school was out, Jenny and I went to Southampton where a close friend owned a summer place. He invited me, along with Jenny and Jon, to spend the summer there with him. I had decorated and furnished the house for him the year before, and loved the peacefulness of the area. One day Jenny looked over at me and said, "Mom, we've been here for three weeks and you haven't been near the ocean once. How come?"

I *had* been avoiding the beach and the ocean, because it reminded me of my grief and loneliness. Yes, it had comforted me and given me strength, and was also where I had felt closest to God. And it was there by the sea that I had often begged God to show me the way, to help me to cope, and in more recent years, to find the daughter I had given up.

But somehow, I did not want to talk to God, right now. I felt too sad to talk about anything and if I went there, I might become too emotional. Besides I did not know what to say to Him. I had already thanked Him for helping me find my daughter, and for getting me through the divorce and finding us a place to live.

Right now, I just couldn't go back to that place of pain.

Instead, I cleaned the house, made new curtains, scrubbed everything in sight, and painted things that did not yet need painting.

At some point I realized what I was really doing: I was trying to wash away the past.

And I was grieving. Grieving for what might have been.

Grieving for the loss of the dream that I once had of a happy family, living the good life that was well within our financial means, but out of our emotional reach.

I thought about those who had come into my life during those years and how they sustained me. I thought of others who I may have rejected because I did not realize they were there to help me.

As our time at the beach went on I came to realize that I had actually grown during those years. As I searched through my life for the meaning of my suffering I found that I had become more compassionate. I also found that I had become more intuitive, and that the more deeply I looked at other people and their situations, the more I saw.

I recognized that I was capable of humor even in the face of negativity. I thought of those people that uplifted me, gave me a sense of worth, a feeling of love, no matter how fleeting. I also found in this time of healing that I was still quite capable of feeling and loving.

Then one day, I finally did go to the sea. Alone, I waded out into the familiar, healing waters of the ocean while waiting for the sun to rise. While I had scrubbed every thing in sight back at the house, attempting to wash away the sadness, I had neglected to wash away my own inner sadness.

I allowed the surf to splash over my body and as wave after wave did its' cleansing, I was able to once more experience the oneness with Nature, God, the Universe.

I swam back, wrapped myself in an oversized towel, and stood ankle deep in the water, watching the sun gently come up over the horizon. Suddenly, I was filled with emotion and I began to cry. I was reminded of a dream I had years ago in McLean, a dream that had great significance to me.

The night of the dream I had awakened suddenly, sitting

bolt upright in bed. Tears were streaming down my face and I could not stop them. I looked over at Charles, who could hear a feather blow across the room, but he was sound asleep, unaware of my sitting up in bed or crying.

In my dream....

I was standing in the surf at the edge of the sea. My daughter, Cara was playing in the sand and oblivious of the storm I saw coming in off the horizon. Before I could get to her and drag her to safety, another storm appeared, and another, and another until there were multiple storms off in the horizon, all forming the spokes in a giant wheel. At first, I was terrified that I might not be able to save my child.

Then I noticed that the center of the large wheel of storms was very bright and suddenly, the spokes of the wheel fanned out, creating a space in the center of the wheel. And there in that space, in the center of the storms, was the beautiful face of our Lord.

I looked at Him and realized He was looking right at me. I cannot begin to describe the beauty of the moment, nor the feeling of peace that flowed through me. I stared at our Lord's face, and reached out, just wanting to touch Him, but the vision slowly began to sink behind the horizon. And as it gently slid behind the sea, it took the form of a glorious sunset, radiating beauty and brightness over the entire area, His loving face still in the center, and then, it was gone.

Awake, I sought the meaning of the dream that was not a dream at all. Almost instantly, I realized that our Lord wanted me to know that He was there, even in the midst of all my storms. I clung to that vision and was strengthened by its message for a long time.

As I looked out at the ocean, and watched the mesmerizing roll and fall of the waves, the memory of this powerful dream reinforced what my heart had come to rely upon... that there is a just, kind, loving, and forgiving God. I was no longer reduced to just *believing* it, I now *knew* it...because He had shown Himself to me.

As I walked back to the beach house, I remembered another similar experience I'd had a few years after this dream. What was significant about this other event was that Charles saw it too, but for some reason, walked away from it.

We were at a Medical meeting at the Homestead Resort in Hot Springs, Virginia, that Spring, and it had been raining for days. After dinner one evening, and before attending a function, Charles suggested we go for a walk. The rain had temporarily stopped and before it started up again, we decided to get some fresh air.

We started up the hill on the main road in front of the resort. It was very dark, the only light coming from the Hotel.

Charles was a good car length ahead of me, and I tried to catch up to him, hoping that in this peaceful atmosphere, away from all the issues at home, we could talk...about what, I couldn't imagine, but hopefully *anything.*

As we walked, the overcast that covered the sky would randomly open and close as the clouds moved and even if you saw a patch of clear sky you could still tell that a downpour was imminent. I could see that the moon was creeping out between some clouds and cast a beautiful light on this very dark path.

Then I heard Charles call back down the hill to me, "Look up at the sky," He said, and he continued to walk up the hill.

I stopped walking and looked up at the opening in the clouds where the moon had cast its light. In the opening, once again, I saw the face of our Lord, as clear as if it were a picture. This was not my imagination. I stared at His beautiful face, unable to take my eyes off of it fearful it would vanish if I did. Then, still fixated on the vision, as more clouds seemed to move out of the way, I saw the entire body of our Lord begin to take shape, down to His feet.

He was draped in a beautiful garment, and I felt an Intense Presence more real than the 'dream' some years before.

I called out, "Charles, turn around and look up at the sky...it's so beautiful!" I don't know if he heard me or if he even looked up, because he did not answer.

But by the time he reached me on his return walk, the vision had disappeared and the clouds were once again filled with the rain that had already begun to fall. "Hurry up," he said, "It's starting to pour," and he ran toward the hotel, with me trailing behind him.

Safe and dry on the porch of the hotel, I asked him why he hadn't stopped to look at the sky after pointing it out to me. "Did you see our Lord's face in the clouds," I asked him.

"Yes, and I saw it first," he said. "Isn't it odd that I saw it before you? I had to point it out to you...you, the holy one."

I was too filled with the beauty, emotion and intense feeling of the moment to even care about Charles' mocking comment to me. I just let it go.

Was the fact that he saw this a confirmation? or, was the vision really intended for him? I wondered.

Back inside the hotel, I was too infused with the experience to be around party-going people, besides, I could not think of one single person in that room to tell about the experience, so I went up to our room alone and tried to recreate it in my mind, then I went to bed.

Back at the beach house, I realized something. Those two incidents had changed forever my belief system. Whatever rules I broke, love was always at the core, and I never intended to harm or hurt anyone. Hopefully, God sees things a little differently than the Church does.

And now I was away from Charles. Away from the old traditional views that told me I was bad and that I must be ashamed of myself.

Whatever it would take to keep moving along this new path, I was...at long last...ready to continue on to a new life.

And so I'd reached, not an end, but truly a new beginning.

As I attempted to find answers over the years, I delved into religion, the early Church, the teachings of the Masters, and came to the conclusion that we had strayed from the basic teachings of Jesus and had forgotten His real message:

"Love one another."

I learned to meditate and *how* to pray effectively. I found that I was missing a lot of information and that some information I *did* have seemed inadequate.

One book that jumped off the shelf was *Wisdom of the Mystic Masters*. We were always told to 'pray', and given prayers to say, but never told *how*. This book was a stepping stone to further learning, and in it, I learned not only the power of prayer, but how to pray more effectively.

I'd used this new way to pray that day by the sea asking for help in locating my child. I'd used it that day in St. James Church when I told God I would do "anything" he asked of me if He would find for me a way out of the marriage.

The first step in effective prayer is to visualize what it is you want...and you must be specific. You don't say, "I need more money." How does the Universe know how much you need, so you say, for example, "I need four thousand dollars."

The next step is to imagine you already have what you are asking for.

Then, you must concentrate on what you have prayed for. Hold this image in your mind for two or three minutes or more without changing the picture.

Then, you must believe, meaning that you have confidence that what you visualize will come to be. If you pray with deep feeling, as I did both times, you add another element to the prayer.

And then, you must completely put it out of your mind. And allow God, or the Universe, or whatever you call the Energy, to manifest.

Through another discipline, I also learned how to protect myself from harmful words and actions. I was taught that by surrounding myself with the White Light of Christ, purely by envisioning it, and knowing it was there, it would reflect back to the sender, whatever was sent to me.

Be it hateful words, or some form of negativity. If it happens to be loving thoughts, they, too, reflect back to the sender as well.

After I learned this technique, I found that the criticism, the mocking words, and the negativity that was slung my way did not have the same effect on me. I still heard the words, but they had lost their power.

Unfortunately, while protecting myself from his words, I had also put a barrier between the two of us.

There are other benefits to this technique. Whenever my children or I travel, I always surround whoever is going, with the White Light of Christ. Many cultures use this symbol but may call it something else. I happen to like the comfort of seeing that White Light surrounding whatever vehicle the person is in.

It is like a blessing, and it was a blessing to me for years.

As I continued to search for answers and meaning, I found Viktor Frankl's book, *Man's Search for Meaning*. Frankl was one of the most gifted psychiatrists in Europe during the sixties. After surviving three years at Auschwitz and other Nazi prisons, he wrote and lectured on the meaning of suffering, and how to preserve the remnants of one's life.

He showed that to survive, one had to find meaning in suffering. While he based his findings on life in the concentration camps, those findings easily transfer to our own lives, because he is talking about human nature.

He showed that to be able to tolerate humiliation, fear, anger at injustice, evil, etc. we must closely guard the images of beloved persons, such as I did of my children.

"We need to have a tie to our religion, develop a sense of humor, and find the healing beauty of nature, however simple or brief the glimpse may be," he said.

I would often leave the house in the evening just long enough to go and watch the sunset, (which was not totally visible from our house). It was healing to me and I could get thru the rest of the evening just by holding the vision of the sunset in my mind.

Frankl reminded me that if there was meaning in life, there was meaning in suffering, but each one of us "must find that meaning for himself."

While "we all have the freedom to change" we do not

always have the freedom from our conditions, but we do have the freedom to "take a stand toward the conditions."

And I found hope in Frankl's belief that "man has the capacity to transcend his predicament and discover an adequate guiding truth."

And the 'guiding truth' of which Victor Frankl spoke, was my belief in a loving, caring, merciful, compassionate God who I loved and Who loved me.

I never doubted that at the right time I would be able to put into action what he was saying. I did find meaning in my suffering, and it was not punishment by God.

The changes in my life did not immediately change the conditions of my life, because the changes were *within* me. As I began to think differently, I began to act differently. I did not realize for a long time my own power. Most importantly, I needed to confront my own truth...who I really was.

My Advice to You

IF I HAVE ANY advice for you, my readers, who find yourself 'stuck' somewhere in life, first, *take care of yourself*. Your health...physical, emotional and spiritual.

Recognize that you are a child of God, no matter how old you are, and if, indeed, we are created in His image and likeness, understand that we have a duty to respect the divine within us, and not allow anyone else to offend that divinity.

Remember, too, that fear is a horrible force to live under, and it comes to you in the form of abusive words and actions.

I always believed Charles' threats were real and that I would be left with nothing...unable to support myself or my children if I left, so I allowed myself to live under the rule of fear.

Some of us stay because we believe we are too unattractive, or old, or that we come with the baggage of children...and no one will want us. Possibly, we have even been told that so we *won't* leave.

If you hate yourself because you see yourself as fearful, possibly cowardly, or as used or unwanted goods...then...find ways to step across that boundary of those lies that are keeping you trapped.

1. Learn how to stand up for yourself.

Find people who have made major changes in their lives or who are strong in the ways you would like to be strong and admire what they have done...Be careful not to compare yourself negatively.

I have a close friend who was marrying for the second time. She had no problem telling her spouse-to-be, who was a bit older, that she wanted to be "left comfortable" in the event he predeceased her, and she wanted to see it in writing.

She has always been able to ask for what she wants and she gets it. Her husband may not like her boldness, but he has always complied with her requests. And even when those requests evolved into demands. *Learn to ask for what you want... others will respect you for it.*

If you know these people you admire, talk to them and make them a part of your healing. Learn the secret of their strength and how they get things done.

2. Do what you have to do to change your belief about yourself.

Examine your core belief about yourself—do you have a shame-based personality, believing that something is intrinsically bad or defective or just wrong about who you are as a human being.

Believing we are defective will undermine us whenever we try to make powerful positive changes on our own behalf.

You must stop believing that you are defective, worthless, bad. Reinforce positive beliefs about yourself and your worth. Look at your accomplishments, find those qualities that you know you possess, even if others ridicule you.

Father Murphy once told me to look in the mirror every day and say to that image, "Know you are loved." And even if *you* do not have a Father Murphy in your life, or *anyone,* there is an unseen Universe that is pure love, so everyday, look at yourself in the mirror, and tell that image, "Know you are loved."

3. Do what it takes to build support.

I was fortunate in having the children's schools, and many of my own Georgetown classmates for support. If you have any friends with whom you can meet regularly, it will re-enforce your feeling of self worth and hopefully, a trust, so that you can voice what is going on in your life.

4. Keep telling people, until someone believes you.

If there is violence in your abusive relationship, have a secret, safe place to go in the event there is danger to you or the children. Keep telling until someone believes you.

And if you think no one knows what goes on behind closed doors, forget it. It is more visible than you think... Sometimes the original family of the abuser is well aware of the abuse, but lives in a world of denial, often blaming the spouse. Still, others are aware, no matter how hard we try to cover up our frightening lives.

This was brought home to me shortly after Charles died in 2004. I was at the funeral of a colleague of his when another physician and his wife stopped to talk to me. We had known each other for years but were not close friends.

The man remarked that he heard through the grapevine that I had been at the hospital every day with Charles when he was dying. "I can't believe you took care of him after the way he treated you all those years." My carefully guarded secret had not been a secret after all. People know, so stop trying to hide the truth...some people do not want to get involved, others do not know what to do, and may just be waiting for you to ask for help.

And, if I have helped even a few of you, then I have found all the meaning I need, in my own suffering.

5. Always remember that *there is way out* but first, you must take possession of yourself.

Stand your ground and defy those who abuse you...they are usually bullies and bullies need to be confronted...they will respect you for it.

WHAT HAPPENED
TO ALL OF US

I WILL NOT TELL the children's stories...they all
have their own, which is why I purposely left their thoughts
out of this memoir, but I *will* tell you what happened to all of
us, and to me in particular.

After the divorce and with my share of the house on
Laburnum Street, I managed to educate two of the three
younger children.

Jenny graduated from the Culinary Institute of America
and had a wonderful, but time-consuming career as a pastry
chef for eleven years. She now is employed by Boeing and is
studying for an additional degree which will enhance not only
her career but her position in the Coast Guard Reserve.

Jon went into the military where he excelled in whatever field he entered. The little boy who was so terrified of
his father, went into Special Operations and was trained to
be *unafraid to die.* He is married and they have three adorable
children. On his own, he has acquired more than one college
degree.

Jeff, who was forced to quit school to support himself after he left home, was able to return to college and graduated with *honors* from UCSD. In addition to owning his own computer programming business, he is also a published author.

Cara, the adored little daughter who could do no wrong, eventually lost favor in her father's eyes, as I knew she would, as soon as she was old enough to contradict or challenge him.

Cara has been a single mom since Dominick, who is now in college, was two. I believe that the absence of a healthy father-daughter relationship has had a strong impact on her life. Still, she has a tremendous ability to deal with adversity and challenge.

After Charles died, she handled his estate beautifully, but the garbled mess took its toll on her and as a result, I promised her I would not ask her to do the same for me.

Matt, the son who was rejected before he was even born, and treated the most badly by Charles, was the kid who not only took care of his father in his final years, but stayed with him the night he died, so "he would not die alone."

Cara and Matt have always supported themselves and both have successful careers.

My daughter, Charlene whom I finally located, has long been integrated into the family and we have a healthy, loving relationship, not only with her, but with her three children. My search for her was the topic of the book I was writing before David asked that I write this one first.

Besides educating two children, I was able to purchase the house I am living in from my share of the proceeds from the sale of the marital home. But not having worked for thirty years and with nothing in my name, I had no credit. In order to get a mortgage, I was required to put 50% down, greatly reducing my cash flow.

As soon as the divorce was final, I found a job in a group OB/GYN office. I worked there for one year when one of the physicians opened his own practice and asked me to go with him. As of this writing, I am still working with him.

Several years ago, I completed a course in Life Coaching which has been helpful both to me and to those I coach. I am also a certified Third Degree Reiki practitioner.

My life is good and I value each day. I thank God for blessing me with wonderful friends and my beautiful family. They have been a tremendous source of comfort and support to me over the years and I love them very much.

I take pride in my home and respect the land it sits on. I am filled with gratitude for all the blessings that have come my way, and if it were not for having written this memoir, I would hardly remember the woman I have been writing about.

God Bless.

ACKNOWLEGEMENTS

I WANT TO THANK David Hazard, who not only encouraged me to write this memoir, but who guided me through it by giving it structure as well as on-going critiquing, saving us countless hours of final editing. His years of experience in the publishing world and his dedication to coaching writers was not only invaluable to me, but made the whole process enjoyable, and I hope to continue working with him in the future. "He who understand you is more kin than a brother."

I am also indebted to Peter Gloege who, with some input from David, designed the book cover and did the page layout. You made my words look attractive. Thank you so much.

I also am indebted to Carol O'Donnell Khalsa who introduced me to David, without whom I probably would never have written the book. I also want to thank her husband, Darshan Khalsa, DoM, whose gentle acupuncture needles have kept my chakras open for many years. Thank both of you for your ongoing encouragement.

I would like to recognize especially those classmates from Georgetown who faithfully stayed in close contact with me over the years. You were my comfort zone and kept me afloat.

 I wrote this book to help others who find themselves trapped in a relationship that is not good. It does not necessarily have to be an abusive relationship, just wrong for them and the fact that they feel trapped. I was aware that by writing such a memoir, I would be taking a risk. Readers might think less of me for how I handled my life and for staying in the relationship as long as I did, but I am willing to risk this to show them a better way. For those who knew or saw my husband in a much better light, it might offend them. But this is not a story about him as much as it is about my life with him, the mistakes I made and how I finally found a way out of decades of abuse.

As a nurse in a Gyn office since 1993, I have seen the results of abused women who are afraid to leave for a variety of reasons. First, their self- esteem goes, and soon the emotional and physical damage becomes evident. It is not my place to counsel them, though a few times I have shared some of my experiences with them. Almost always, when they leave the damaging relationship, their physical symptoms go away as well.

I did not want the book to be depressing… I wanted it to be a source of hope. You *can* recover your self-image and heal from the wounds. And no matter your age, if you follow the suggestions in the last chapter, you will be ready to start your new life much sooner.

Nancy Hannan

17985197R00094

Made in the USA
Lexington, KY
08 October 2012